SKYE

SKYE

NORMAN NEWTON

PEVENSEY

ISLAND GUIDES

The Pevensey Press is an imprint of
David & Charles

First published 1995
Reprinted 1997, 1998, 2001

Map on page 6 by David Langworth

ISBN 0 907115 89 6

Designed and typeset by
Drum & Company
and printed in Hong Kong
by Wing King Tong Co Ltd
for David & Charles
Brunel House   Newton Abbot
Devon

CONTENTS

Left: Cuillin Hills and Loch Harport

Half title: top left: River Sligachan, the old bridge and Glamaig, site of the annual race to the top and back; top right: Kilt Rock and waterfall; bottom: Dunvegan Castle

Title page: Across Loch Snizort from Bernisdale

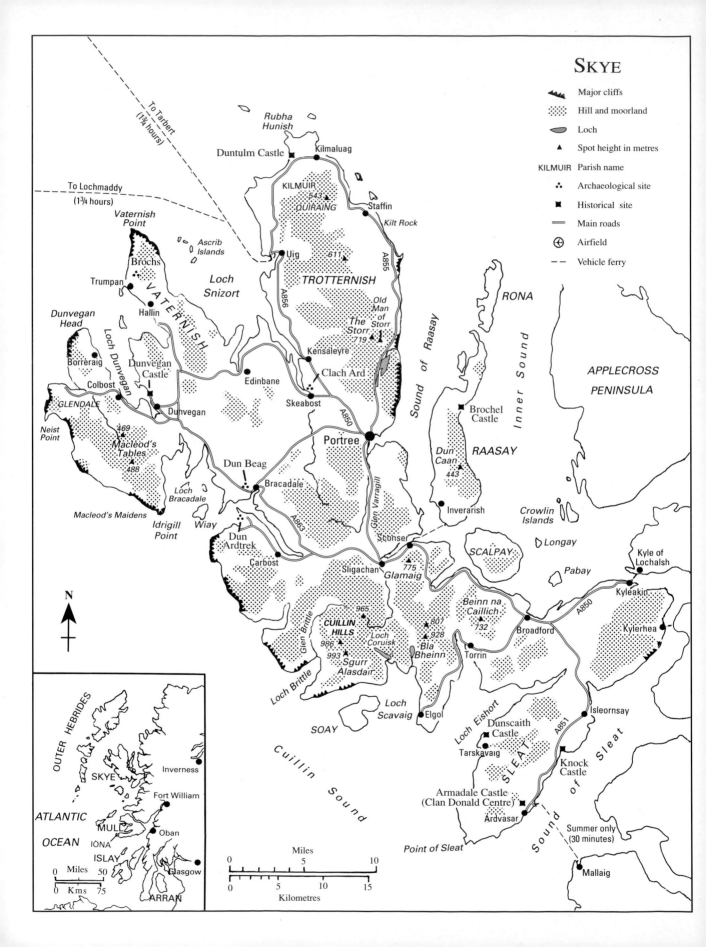

SKYE

Major cliffs
Hill and moorland
Loch
Spot height in metres
KILMUIR Parish name
Archaeological site
Historical site
Main roads
Airfield
Vehicle ferry

To Tarbert
(1¾ hours)

To Lochmaddy
(1¾ hours)

Rubha Hunish

Duntulm Castle
Kilmaluag

KILMUIR
543 ▲
QUIRAING
Staffin
Kilt Rock
A855

Vaternish Point
Ascrib Islands

Uig
611 ▲
A856

Brochs
TROTTERNISH

Trumpan
Loch Snizort
VATERNISH
Hallin

RONA

Dunvegan Head
Loch Dunvegan
Old Man of Storr
The Storr
719 ▲

Borreraig
Dunvegan Castle
Edinbane
Kensaleyre

APPLECROSS PENINSULA

Colbost
Dunvegan
Skeabost
Clach Ard

Brochel Castle

GLENDALE
A850

Neist Point
469 ▲
Macleod's Tables
488 ▲

Portree

Dun Caan
443 ▲
RAASAY

Inner Sound

Dun Beag
Bracadale

Sound of Raasay

Loch Bracadale

Glen Varragill

Inverarish

Crowlin Islands

Macleod's Maidens
Idrigill Point
Wiay

Dun Ardtrek
Carbost

A863

Sligachan
Sc…ser
775 ▲
Glamaig

SCALPAY

Longay
Pabay

Kyle of Lochalsh

Glen Brittle

CUILLIN HILLS
965 ▲
986 ▲
993 ▲
Sgurr Alasdair

Loch Coruisk
807 ▲
928 ▲
Bla Bheinn

Beinn na Caillich
732 ▲

Broadford

A850

Kyleakin

Kylerhea

Torrin

SOAY
Loch Scavaig
Elgol

Loch Eishort

Dunscaith Castle
Tarskavaig

SLEAT
A851

Isleornsay

Knock Castle

Loch Brittle

Cuillin Sound

Armadale Castle
(Clan Donald Centre)
Ardvasar

Sound of Sleat

Point of Sleat

Summer only
(30 minutes)

Mallaig

N

Miles
0   5   10
Kilometres
0   5   10   15

OUTER HEBRIDES

ATLANTIC OCEAN

SKYE
Inverness
Fort William

MULL
IONA
Oban
ISLAY
Glasgow
ARRAN

Miles
0   50
Kms
0   75

INTRODUCTION TO THE MISTY ISLE:
PENINSULAS AND SEA-LOCHS

The island of Skye (in Gaelic, An t-Eilean Sgitheanach) is the largest of the Inner Hebrides, part of an archipelago scattered like jewels in the western ocean off the west coast of Scotland. Skye is surprisingly large: 535sq miles (1,385sq km), with a complicated topography comprising fingers of land separated by sea-lochs penetrating far inland, forming 350 miles (563km) of coastline. Loch Snizort, Loch Dunvegan, Loch Harport, Loch Eishort, Loch Ainort, Loch Sligachan – the names reveal the mixture of Norse and Gaelic culture which has influenced the island over many centuries.

It is possible to run up a hefty mileage during a week's holiday in Skye; the island is 50 miles (80km) long and from 7 to 25 miles (11 to 40 km) broad, with an extensive road system penetrating to all but the most remote corners. On the other hand it is just as easy to fall in love with one part of the island and spend all your time there, exploring its landscape and its past.

Above: View across the Sound of Sleat to the mainland from near Isleornsay

Above: The ruined chapel of Cill Chriosd, near Torrin. Below: Skye ferry at Kyleakin

This book guides you through the whole island, district by district, pausing from time to time to give some background information on the history, wildlife, mountains, climate, natural environment and traditions of Skye. There is lots to see and lots to do, and many visitors return to Skye again and again, never tiring of its constantly changing landscapes as weather patterns reveal nuances of light and shade that cause even the locals to pause and be grateful that they live in such an awesomely beautiful place. It can be harsh and unforgiving too, and not just in winter – anybody planning excursions in the hills and mountains should be well prepared, and aware that they are in some of the most challenging and demanding wilderness in Europe.

History is all around, in the form of castles, prehistoric forts and ancient burial cairns. There is a pervasive awareness of the past, and most local people will have stories of clan battles, Danish princesses and folk heroes, because Skye has been a battleground for thousands of years, a place where different peoples mixed and often clashed, before settling down to live in harmony. This book does not attempt to fill in *all* the fascinating and interesting details of the past, but we hope we provide enough to whet your appetite and make you want to know more. You can find out more about Skye either by reading more about it – a reading list is provided at the end of the book – or just by being there and exploring the island, and talking to people; either of these approaches can be very rewarding. Hundreds of books have been written about Skye, as visitors feel the need to share their enjoyment with others; they have been doing this since the eighteenth century, so their efforts provide a useful record of island society. And as for exploring Skye, it is the task of a lifetime to do it thoroughly, and you will never run out of surprises.

In this book we try to give you enough background – enough of an appetite – to make your visit more enjoyable; though in the end it is up to each person to make the most of the opportunities he finds – for example, by taking advantage of good weather and making the most of the long summer days, for in the summer months it is still light until nearly midnight, and the early mornings are a magical time.

Skye is an ideal holiday destination for many different kinds of people. If you are a car tourist, there are roads to most parts of the island, and if you actually like driving, you will find some of the most challenging roads in Britain. If you are more energetic, you will find that Skye's reputation as a mecca for climbers and hill-walkers is well deserved. Skye is a mountainous island, but cyclists should not be too deterred by that, for most of the roads keep to the valley floors, or after an initial climb, traverse relatively flat moorland.

All those interested in the natural environment will find themselves fully occupied, and likely to enjoy experiences they will remember for a lifetime. Although Skye is a big island, it is not necessary to have your own transport to get around it as there are

Old Man of Storr and Loch Fada

bus services to most townships, and these routes can often be linked up by interesting walks across country. No part of the island is more than five miles from the sea, so the scenery is superb, with constantly changing combinations of mountains and sea lochs.

Geologically Skye is renowned for its lava landscapes, especially in the Trotternish area where the Old Man of Storr and the unusual formations of the Quiraing would not be out of place in a lunar landscape, and attract many visitors. Also greatly admired, whenever they are visible through the ubiquitous mist, are the Cuillin, jagged mountains of hard gabbro that provide the best climbing in Britain, summer and winter. The Red Cuillins, consisting of only slightly less hard granite, have eroded into more rounded shapes and have slopes of scree. The unexpected fertility of some parts of the island derives from underlying sandstones and limestones which surface around the volcanic rocks.

Skye has a rich and varied range of archaeological and historical monuments, testimony to its long and often turbulent history. Of particular interest are the brochs of Dun Ardtreck, near Carbost, and Dun Beag, just west of Bracadale, both of which were very neatly built with square-sided facing-stones. These ruins were originally stone towers up to 30ft (9m) high, masterpieces of Iron Age architecture, with hollow, double-skinned walls to lessen the weight and make the great height possible.

Skye is part of the heartland of Gaelic culture, with a large proportion of the population of 8,500 speaking the Gaelic language in everyday life. As in other parts of the Hebrides, this culture is under threat, in particular because there are so many incomers, but there is a resurrection of interest in Gaelic culture which is assisted by a Gaelic college (Sabhal Mor Ostaig), Gaelic poetry (for example Sorley Maclean), Gaelic rock music (Run Rig), a winning shinty team, a radical local newspaper (*The West Highland Free Press*), also economic support from Highlands and Islands Enterprise, and spiritual underpinning from the Sabbatarian Free Church. Museums and heritage centres, for example at Luib, Colbost, Glendale, Kilmuir, Portree and Armadale, help to interpret crofting society and island history to visitors.

The Museum at Luib

The 'Skye Boat Song', beloved of generations of Scottish school children and therefore sung in the farthest corners of the English-speaking world, commemorates the visit of Bonnie Prince Charlie to Skye. In Kilmuir burial ground is the grave of Flora MacDonald and a monument to her, the most famous lady in Skye's long history. The monument has Dr Johnson's epitaph engraved on it: 'Her name will be mentioned in history and if courage and fidelity be virtues, mentioned with honour'. It was she who helped Bonnie Prince Charlie to escape capture after the defeat of his army at Culloden in 1746, by transporting him in a boat from North Uist, 'over the sea to Skye'. After Flora's part in the prince's escape became known, she was arrested and spent almost a year in the Tower of London. After a busy life, including some twelve years in North Carolina, she returned to her husband's house at Kingsburgh; she died in Skye in 1790, and it is said that her funeral was the largest ever witnessed in the Highlands.

Another aspect of the romance of the island's past is represented in the same Kilmuir graveyard, as members of the MacArthur family, hereditary pipers to the MacDonalds at Duntulm Castle, are buried there. Kilmuir also has a major visitor attraction in the restored thatched cottages that make up the Skye Museum of Island Life, opened in 1965. Here the way of life of a traditional crofting community of the past can be experienced in its original landscape.

The most famous Skye piping family were the MacCrimmons of Borreraig, hereditary pipers to the MacLeods of Dunvegan for over two hundred years. They ran a college of piping, with a course of instruction that

Dancer competing in the Highland Games, Portree

Top left: Dun Beag

Bottom left: Flora MacDonald's grave at Kilmuir, Trotternish

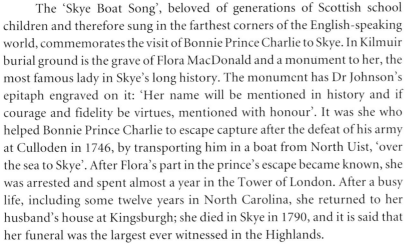

lasted for three years. A cairn commemorates their activities, and every year in August a special piping competition is held in their honour in the drawing-room of Dunvegan Castle. Classical piping music, traditionally played only by the greatest pipers, is known as 'pibroch' or *piobaireachd*, or *Ceol mor*, 'the great music', pronounced 'kyoll more'. A new piping centre at the old school in Borreraig tells the story of the bagpipes, which survived their banning after Culloden to become the internationally recognised symbol of the Highland Scot.

In the nineteenth century the native culture came under serious threat when an estimated thirty thousand islanders emigrated between 1840 and 1888. In 1882 was the Battle of the Braes, a confrontation over grazing rights between local farmers in the Braes district near Portree and fifty Glasgow policemen who were imported to keep control. After a pitched battle, gunboats were sent and a force of marines landed at Uig. However there was a public outcry and as a result a Royal Commission was established by Gladstone; the outcome was the Crofters Act of 1886 which provided security of tenure at a fair and controlled rent. This system, which replaced the original communal townships, remains in force today.

Early maps of Skye show just how difficult it was for cartographers to grasp the complicated topography of the island's peninsulas. On Ptolemy's map of Britain, produced in the second century AD, the western coastline and islands of Scotland are barely recognisable to anyone accustomed to modern Ordnance Survey maps. Amongst the islands he indicated was *Ocitis*, printed in the Middle Ages as *Scitis* and believed to represent Skye. It is thought that the information used by Ptolemy was collected by the Roman fleet which sailed round the coasts of Scotland in about AD85 in support of Agricola's invading armies. His son-in-law Tacitus, described the western coasts of Scotland in terms which very much call to mind the waters around the island of Skye:

> Nowhere has the sea a wider dominion; it has many currents running in every direction; it does not merely flow and ebb within the limits of the shore, but penetrates and winds far inland, and finds a home among hills and mountains as though in its own domain.

The first to describe the island of Skye in any detail was Donald Monro, Dean of the Isles, who travelled round the Hebrides in the course of his work in the 1540s and published his account under the title *A Description of the Western Isles of Scotland called Hybrides* in 1549. This is an important source at a time when facts are hard to come by; his pages devoted to Skye have a remarkable number of facts combined with a close economy of words. He assists his readers to place Skye on their mental map of the Hebrides by observing quaintly that it is 'two miles north of Soa', or Soay – 'sheep island' – which is perhaps like saying that Britain is two miles north of the Isle of Wight! He wrote:

Pipers at the Highland Games

North fra the ile Soabrettill lyes the grate ile of Skye, tending from the south to the north to fortey twa myles, roughe and hard land; that is to say from the south poynt of Sleitt to the north poynt of Trouternesse, and eight myle braid in some places and in uther places twelve myles braid.

He refers to the mountains, the fertility of the land for growing oats and pasture, the woods, forests, deer, game and salmon. He mentions the castles and their owners, describing Dunvegan as 'the castle of Dunbeggan pertaining to McCloyd of Herray, ane starke strengthe, biggit upon ane craig'.

The first map to show the island as even vaguely like its actual shape was published in Blaeu's 1654 atlas of Scotland, based on an actual survey carried out by Timothy Pont between the years 1585 and 1595. In the preface to Blaeu's atlas Pont's experiences are described rather dramatically:

> . . . he travelled on foot right through the whole of this kingdom, as no one before him had done; he visited all the islands, occupied for the most part by inhabitants hostile and uncivilised, and with a language different from our own; being often stripped . . . by fierce robbers.

We owe Timothy Pont a great debt for his mapmaking endeavours, but we also have to acknowledge that he was responsible for establishing a view of Hebrideans which very nearly resulted in genocide in later centuries.

Hermann Moll, a Dutchman living in London, produced a better map of Skye in 1725, but the first 'modern' map did not appear until 1824, and did not become widely available until it was published in John Thomson's *Atlas of Scotland* in

Farm at Torrin, with Blaven behind

1832; however, it can be regarded as the ancestor of today's Ordnance Survey maps. In 1819 the geologist John MacCulloch produced a geological map of Skye, but with the coastline much distorted; in fact the colouring of the geological features is both hard to follow and to match with modern interpretations of Skye's underlying rocks, an aspect of the island's constitution which is so interesting for visiting parties of university geology students.

Loch Bay and Stein with Harris beyond

TIDES AND CURRENTS

THE WATERS ROUND SKYE present a real challenge to sailors by reason of their innumerable hazards and the vagaries of the many currents and tide-races. The tidal stream between Kylerhea and the mainland at Glenelg flows like a river in spate; this strait is the narrowest passage between the mainland and Skye, but to cross or pass through this channel, particularly before the days of steam, was a hazardous undertaking.

Shipping around Scotland's west coast and among the islands is still to a great extent governed by the highly intricate tidal system of these waters; some of the tidal streams are so strong and turbulent that they cannot be ignored even by modern power-driven ships. Every summer sees the local coastguard stretched to the limit by southern sailors who have never experienced anything like it, and who find themselves admiring the Roman

admiral who braved these coasts so long ago, without modern navigating aids. The Vikings in their longships succeeded in mastering these dangerous seas, and the local boatmen who have inherited their homesteads still possess that essential and detailed local knowledge which can often become a matter of survival. Currents and tides can be erratic and unpredictable, depending very much on wind direction and local conditions. Local knowledge of these conditions has given inhabitants the advantage over foreign invaders – including sometimes dangerously naive modern yachtsmen.

As well as the constantly changing weather patterns, the other main influences on tides and currents are the irregular coastline, the uneven sea bottom, and the many small islands scattered throughout these waters. Anybody thinking of navigating in this area must acquire the *West of Scotland Pilot*, an absolutely indispensable guide to tides, currents and anchorages.

GETTING THERE

The ferry at Kyleakin making one of its last journeys before the opening of the road bridge

TRAVELLING TO SKYE is easier now than at any time in the past, and it is now the most accessible Hebridean island. The opening of the Skye road bridge in 1995, replacing the short ferry crossing between Kyle of Lochalsh and Kyleakin, is the most revolutionary development to hit Skye for many centuries, with somewhat unpredictable results. Skye residents welcome the improved convenience of being able to drive on and off the island at any time, although for the last few years there has been a twenty-four-hour ferry service at Kyle. They do, however, resent having to pay a toll, currently fixed at the same level as the ferry tickets, so the bridge has brought no financial savings, although locals can still buy books of tickets at a discounted price.

Naturally there is some apprehension that Skye will become just another day-trip for mainland tourists, with a detrimental effect on bed-and-breakfast trade, but the authorities seem sure that the new bridge will bring increased advantages all round, from which the island will gain economically. It is less sure that the social effects will be so unambiguously beneficial. The issue is very political, and a change of government nationally could very well bring a more radical approach, perhaps making the bridge toll-free but allowing Caledonian MacBrayne to keep its ferry running, maybe as a seasonal alternative to tourists who still value travelling '*over* the sea to Skye', instead of well above it.

On the Skye ferry looking back to the Kyle of Lochalsh

Kyleakin has always been the traditional port of entry to Skye. The crossing from the railhead at Kyle of Lochalsh was a short, five-minute one, with a frequent service interrupted only by the wildest storms. This is where the Norwegian King Haakon anchored his longships in 1263, on his way to the fiasco of the Battle of Largs; the place-name 'Kyleakin' bears his name. However there are several other

Boat at Loch Slapin

ways of getting to Skye. A few miles to the south is a seasonal ferry connection from Glenelg on the mainland to Kylerhea, another short crossing through treacherous, tidal races. This route is attractive to the more leisurely traveller with an interest in history. At Glenelg are the remains of the Bernera Barracks, built to hold a Hanoverian garrison after the Jacobite rebellions in the eighteenth century, while in the nearby glen are two of the best preserved brochs – Iron Age drystone fortress towers – in Scotland.

At the southern end of the Sleat (pronounced 'slate') peninsula a ferry connects Armadale to Mallaig, another mainland railhead, with connections through Fort William to Glasgow and London. This ferry only takes vehicles in the summer, but operates as a passenger service for the rest of the year. On summer Sundays, Calmac operates a service from Mallaig to Kyle, aimed principally at tourists.

At the opposite end of Skye, from the harbour of Uig in the Trotternish peninsula, there are ferry connections to the Outer Hebrides (Tarbert, Harris and Lochmaddy, North Uist). These routes can be incorporated into Calmac's 'Island Hopscotch' scheme, with considerable savings on offer.

Another short crossing connects Sconser on Skye to the island of Raasay; this will be described separately in Chapter 7.

A QUICK TOUR

FROM KYLEAKIN there is a good, fast, new road to Broadford, a lively village of 900 people, with craft shops and an annual folk festival. From here a scenic road leads eventually to Elgol, from where there is a fine view of the Cuillin ridge. Just before Broadford another road turns south to the Sleat peninsula, winding its way down to the ferry pier at Armadale.

Portree Harbour

From Broadford the main road to Portree follows the coast to the head of Loch Ainort and then climbs steeply beneath Lord MacDonald's Forest and Glamaig to Loch Sligachan, then through Glen Varragill to Portree. There are fantastic views of the sea-lochs and offshore islands.

Portree, with a population of over 1,000, is the main town, with hotels, shops, banks and all the usual services, including a Tourist Information Centre. Its name derives from the visit of King James V in 1540, on an expedition to quell insurrections among the rebellious population of the Western Isles. In this aim he was not notably successful.

The harbour at Portree is not as busy as it once was, but is still a working fishing port. The harbour itself is a fine natural haven, deep and protected from the fiercest storms. If Portree had possessed a well-populated hinterland for an export or import trade, this could have been one of the busiest ports in the Western Isles. Behind the pier with its attractive row of shops, cottages and small hotels, the ground rises to the finger of land known as 'the Lump', which divides the harbour from Loch Portree. The building prominent above the harbour is Meall House, the oldest building in the town, once used as a prison but now the Tourist Information Centre. Here can be found all kinds of brochures and leaflets, mostly free, explaining the wide range of activities and services available on the island.

From Portree the road system diverges in all directions: first, to the north is the Trotternish peninsula, which has a road right round its coastline, and a small connecting road over the moor from Uig to Staffin. Right at the north of Trotternish is Duntulm, a historic and picturesque castle ruin, not to be missed.

To the south-west of Portree is Minginish, reached either by a moor-

Loch Cill Chriosd

land road to Loch Harport or by a road turning off through Glen Drynoch at Sligachan. Climbers, hill-walkers, hostellers and serious mountaineering types head to Glen Brittle in Minginish, while thirsty car-tourists may be tempted beyond Carbost to Talisker, to the distillery there.

In the north-west part of the island there are two more peninsulas, Duirinish and Waternish (or Vatternish). The peninsulas are separated by Loch Dunvegan, at the head of which is the world-famous MacLeod stronghold, Dunvegan Castle, an ancient fortress still lived in by the chief of Clan MacLeod. On the western edge of Duirinish is Neist Point, with its lighthouse (now automated). From the road above the headland there are panoramic and dramatic views of the sea-cliffs and the far-off Outer Hebrides across the Minch – look out for supertankers waiting to cause another ecological superdisaster.

After this whirlwind tour of the 'Misty Isle' (in Gaelic, Eilean a'Cheo) it is time to embark on a more leisurely exploration of the different districts of Skye, starting with the area most visitors will encounter first after they have whizzed over the new toll bridge.

Overleaf: Neist Point, Duirinish

1 Over the Sea to Skye?
Kyleakin, Broadford and Elgol

Kyleakin

Kyleakin

THE VILLAGE OF KYLEAKIN will have to come to terms with the fact that with the new toll bridge across the narrow straits from the mainland it is no longer the teeming ferry terminal that it once was. Nevertheless, it has its attractions and its appeal. Just on the east edge of the village is Castle Moil (in Gaelic, Caisteal Maol 'the bare castle'), the first of Skye's many castles that visitors encounter but which is now a dangerous ruin. It has a long and fascinating history: in the fifteenth century it was a stronghold of the Mackinnons, but references to 'Dunakin' (Haakon's Fort) suggest an earlier history, and indeed there are traces of a possibly tenth-century building, with walls nearly ten feet thick. Tradition says that the castle was built by a Norwegian princess, 'Saucy Mary' who married a Mackinnon chief and collected tolls from ships passing through the straits, helped by a massive chain stretched across to the mainland.

Traditions are not always literally true, but it is disconcerting to find a precedent for charging tolls at Kyleakin!

In the Middle Ages Skye was part of the territory of the Lords of the Isles, the MacDonald lineage who ruled the Hebrides and the western coasts of Scotland as a sea-kingdom. The Lordship was forfeited by James IV in 1493 after years of skirmishing between the Scottish Crown and various clan chieftains, but when he was killed in 1513 at the battle of Flodden, along with most of the Scottish nobility, there seemed to be a window of opportunity to re-establish the MacDonald Lordship in the Isles. A meeting of everybody with an interest in the subject was held at 'Dunakin', and they resolved to support Sir Donald MacDonald of Lochalsh as their leader. The true heir to the Lords of the Isles, Donald Dubh, was imprisoned in Edinburgh Castle and the rebellion soon fizzled out, as did several other attempts to recreate the glories of past days.

Donald Dubh himself escaped from captivity in 1545 and raised the MacDonald standard in Islay and the west, but when he died of a fever at Drogheda in Ireland the following year his followers once again disintegrated and there were to be no further attempts to restore the Lordship of the Isles – although of course some historians see the Jacobite rebels of 1715 and 1745 as harking back to these days. Donald Monro, Dean of the Isles, mentions Castle Moil in 1549: 'the castill at DunnaKynne pertaining to MacKynnoun'.

The castle itself stands on a knoll of Torridonian sandstone, though it has suffered severely from neglect and the ravages of time. In 1949 a large chunk of its western side collapsed, as did a large portion of the north wall in 1989. Recent consolidation work undertaken by Historic Scotland has attempted to render the remaining ruins safe. One benefit of the collapse was that in 1951 a hoard of medieval coins was found in the masonry of the west wall, mostly dating from the reign of James VI.

At Kyleakin and Broadford the visitor first encounters the so-called 'raised beaches' that are such a feature of coastal scenery in the Hebrides. These are evidence of a time when sea-level was higher than it is today, and they are an important part of Skye's geological history; they occur at different levels and date from different times, but all are the result of changes in sea-level caused by the last Ice Age. From 20000BC when the ice began to melt seriously until soon after 8000BC when the first Mesolithic hunter-gatherers appeared on the scene there were several variations in sea-level. When the ice first melted, which was a fairly rapid process, sea-level rose, and waves crashed into the land at a higher level, forming cliffs and beaches.

However, with the great weight of ice removed from the land – it was over a mile thick – the land actually began gradually to rise . This process, known as 'isostatic recovery', eventually had the result of leaving the post-glacial beaches high and dry. They came in handy much later for road-makers! They also provide a relatively well-drained, sandy, fertile strip along the coastline.

SKYE ROAD RULES

As you travel rapidly along the road to Broadford, look out for the remains of older roads, some of which were in use until the 1970s. It is certainly a lot easier these days to bring a motor vehicle to Skye, but the pace of change, although rapid, has not been equal throughout the island, so be prepared for some very narrow, twisty, single-track roads in some of the remoter parts. These roads are very much a feature of island life, but they do seem to give rise to much misunderstanding and not a little aggravation, so it is worth considering here a few basic rules of behaviour. Passing places on single-track roads are marked with black and white poles; as well as allowing approaching vehicles to pass safely, these should be used to allow following vehicles to overtake. If you meet a bus or a truck, you may have to reverse to the nearest passing place: despite the improved power of modern internal combustion engines, it is still considered courteous to give way to traffic travelling up-hill. Locals are often in more of a hurry than tourists to get where they are going, and do not appreciate dawdlers – don't get upset therefore if a car following you honks its horn and flashes its lights: it could be a local doctor on the way to an emergency.

NORSE NAMES

The influence of the long Norse occupation of Skye – it lasted for three hundred and fifty years – is well illustrated by the survival to this day of many place-names which are Norse in origin. For example the -bost ending in place-names signifies a Norse bolstadr or homestead, often preceded by a Norse personal name; thus Carbost is named after the homestead of a Norse farmer called Kari, and Orbost after Orri. The -nish ending is the Norse for a 'ness' or headland, while -aig is from the Norse vik, a bay; furthermore these elements are also often combined with personal names: Toravaig is 'Thori's Bay', Trotternish is 'Thrond's Headland'. Bearreraig is 'Bjorn's Bay', Hinnisdal is 'Hengist's Dale', Aulavaig is 'Olaf's Bay' – there are dozens of examples. Examples of Norse names surviving to the present day in both surnames and forenames include MacLeod, MacAskill, Tolmie, MacIvor, MacAulay, Gunn, MacCrae, and Tormod (anglicised as Norman), Torquil (Thor's Kettle, referring to a whirlpool or similar feature), Godfrey (Godred), and Ranald or Reginald (from the Latin version of Rögnvaldr, written by Gaelic speakers as Raghnaill). Somerled's name, too, has many versions, some still in use: it comes from the Norse sumar-lidi 'summer-traveller' (or Viking), rendered as 'Somhairle' in Gaelic, pronounced and anglicised as 'Sorley'. There are many strands to Skye's history and to its people, which sometimes take a fair bit of unravelling!

VIKINGS

BEFORE LEAVING KYLEAKIN let us take a little time to consider who Haakon was, why this particular 'kyle' (in Gaelic, *caol* 'strait or narrows') was named after him, and the effects of the Norse occupation of Skye. Viking raiders, followed by Norse settlers, first started coming to the island soon after AD800. Initially they raided Christian monasteries, looted their treasures, murdered their priests, and made off with the island's most valuable commodity, slaves (many of whom ended up in the new Norse colonies in Iceland and Greenland). Later they came in their hundreds in their longships with stock, seed corn and their families, to establish homesteads. Eventually they intermarried with the 'native' population, producing in their children a particularly fearsome combination of temperaments. There were, of course, initial battles and skirmishes as local island populations resisted the new settlers, who took the best land – and, one suspects, the best women – for themselves. But things settled down, and in many parts of the Hebrides, including Skye, the two communities co-existed until they became almost indistinguishable. We shall see their influence, for example, in the Clan MacLeod, a lineage of Norse origin which came to own and rule all of Skye and a lot more besides.

By the 1090s the Norse overlordship of the Western Isles was apparently getting a little shaky because the Norwegian king, Magnus Barefoot, came over with expeditions in successive years to re-impose his authority. His raids on various islands, including Skye, are described in sagas in bloodcurdling language which make it abundantly clear that any ideas of local autonomy would not be tolerated:

> When Magnus came to the Hebrides he began at once to plunder and burn the inhabited lands, and he slew the menfolk. And they robbed everything wherever they went. The people of the land fled far and wide; some to Scotland's firths, some south to Kintyre, or over to Ireland. Some received quarter and did homage.
>
> The branch-scorcher played greedily up into the sky in Lewis; flame spouted from the houses. The King made red the sword of battle. The farmers lost life and wealth.
>
> The diminisher of the battle-gosling's hunger caused Skye to be plundered: the glad wolf reddened tooth in many a mortal wound upon Tiree. The Scots-expeller went mightily; the people of Mull ran to exhaustion. Greenland's King caused maids to weep, south in the islands.
>
> (*Heimskringla Saga*)

All in all, not a pleasant experience for the people of Skye and the other islands of the Hebrides. So when Somerled of Argyll led an insurrection against Olaf of the Isle of Man, the Norse overlord of the area in the 1150s, he found widespread support. Somerled (who had a Celtic father and a Norse mother) defeated Olaf's forces in a sea battle off Islay in 1156, establishing the lineage which eventually took the name MacDonald, after his grandson.

The Lords of the Isles ran the Hebrides as a semi-autonomous sea-kingdom until 1263, when King Haakon of Norway again attempted to restore Norse control; this may have been partly as a result of an appeal from the people of Skye who had been raided by the Lord of the Isles as part of his campaign to assert his claim to the earldom of Ross. Haakon anchored his fleet of longships at Kyleakin in 1263, then sailed on down the west coast, mustering further help from local chieftains. He sailed up the Firth of Clyde and opened negotiations with the Scottish king. These dragged on and on, as negotiations do, until political events were overtaken by the weather. Autumn gales blew some of Haakon's fleet across the Clyde from their anchorage in Lamlash Bay on the east coast of Arran, and a few ships were blown ashore at Largs, where the excited land armies of the Scottish king engaged them in skirmishes along the beach. This was the overrated Battle of Largs, of which the major significance lay not in a massive defeat inflicted by Scottish forces (which did not happen) but in the fact that Haakon had to withdraw without achieving his aims.

Castle Moil and the Skye ferry

Haakon visited Skye again on his way north, resupplying his fleet at 'Vestrafjord', the name in the sagas for Loch Bracadale. He died, of old age and possibly exhaustion after a long and unfulfilling campaign, in the Orkneys on his way back home. Three years later, in 1266, his successor negotiated a political settlement with Scotland, ceding all Norse possessions in the Western Isles to Alexander III. Needless to say, the Lords of the Isles took a dim view of this arrangement, and continued to act as if they were the legal authority in the islands until these were finally forfeited in the reign of James IV, in 1493.

The development of Kyleakin as the island's main ferry terminal received a boost with the arrival of the Highland Railway at Kyle of Lochalsh in 1897. As early as 1616 and again in 1627 Lachlan MacKinnon of Castle Moil at Kyleakin held charters for his lands as a barony, with rights to operate and maintain a ferry boat on the Kyle. But in earlier times this meant Kylerhea, and not Kyleakin.

KYLERHEA

THE ROAD TO KYLERHEA turns off the main road halfway between Kyleakin and Broadford. You would never think it now, but this was once the most important route into Skye. The reason? The cattle trade, which was the mainstay of the island economy from medieval times until well into the twentieth century. It was this trade that led to the development of roads on the island, establishing routes which we career along today. All the islands in the Western Isles produced cattle, but those close to the mainland had a big advantage. Skye cattle were gathered together at 'trysts' on the island at Portree, Sligachan and Broadford, and driven over 'drove' roads to Kylerhea, where they were *swum* across the narrows to the mainland and taken on to the great lowland markets, of which the most important was at Falkirk. There they were traded for barley, oats and other necessities which could not be grown in the quantities required on the island itself. In *The Wealth of Nations*, Adam Smith explains the basic economics of this:

> Live cattle are, perhaps, the only commodity of which the transportation is more expensive by sea than by land. By land they carry themselves to market. By sea, not only the cattle, but their food and water too, must be carried at no small expense and inconveniency.

The cattle trade was of great importance to the island, and apart from a few sheep and during the Napoleonic wars the sale of kelp, it was Skye's main source of money. This must have been obvious to the Amsterdam mapmaker Blaeu in 1654 when he published and engraved the map of Skye prepared by Timothy Pont, for in the top right-hand corner of the map a striking decoration was engraved showing a scene of drovers and cattle.

The main drove roads in Skye carried the island's own exports of cattle, as well as those brought over from Lochboisdale, Lochmaddy, Rodel and Tarbert in the Outer Isles. The main drove roads through Skye ran from Loch Pooltiel, Dunvegan and Uig, with a northern route passing through Portree to Sligachan where it joined the southern route which had passed through Bracadale. From Sligachan the road ran on to Kylerhea, being joined at Broadford by a road from Strathaird. The export of cattle from Skye in substantial numbers began before 1500.

The fact that the Western Highlands and Islands of Scotland were the main breeding grounds for cattle is chiefly an accident of geography. The remote west and particularly the islands escaped much of the civil strife and upheaval to which the rest of Scotland was subjected. Skye was also particularly favoured by its comparatively mild oceanic climate, which saved it from the severer frosts and snow of the mainland and stimulated a better and richer growth of grass. This put a 'bloom' on the beasts which made them particularly attractive to dealers from England and the south of Scotland

Right: Beinn na Caillich and Loch Cill Chriosd

who, as the trade grew and flourished, came north in greater and greater numbers to Skye and the other islands to buy. The quality of the cattle was commented upon by George Culley towards the end of the eighteenth century, when he wrote:

> It is in the Northern and Western Highlands and all the Islands and particularly the Isle of Skye and that tract of country near Kintail that you meet with the native breed of Kyloes; a hardy, industrious and excellent breed of cattle calculated in every respect to thrive in a cold, exposed mountainous country.

After passing through the island markets or trysts, the cattle were taken across to the mainland at Kylerhea; this dangerous strait was the main crossing-point until the railway arrived at Kyle of Lochalsh in 1897. Various writers, among them the Welsh eighteenth-century tourist Thomas Pennant, Martin Martin of Skye, John Knox the bookseller and even Daniel Defoe, have described the ferrying of the beasts across Kyle Rhea. A good account is in the 1813 Agricultural Survey of Inverness-shire, which gives considerable detail of how it was done;

> All the cattle reared in the Isle of Skye which are sent to the southern markets pass from the island to the mainland by the Caol Rea. Their numbers are very considerable, by some supposed to be over 5,000, by others 8,000 annually . . . they are forced to swim over Caol Rea. For this purpose the drovers purchase ropes which are cut at the length of 3 feet having a noose at one end. This noose is put round the under jaw of every cow, taking care to leave the tongue free. The reason given for leaving the tongue loose is that the animal may be able to keep the salt water from going down its throat in such a quantity as to fill all the cavities in the body which would prevent the action of the lungs . . . Then every cow is tied to the tail of the cow before until a string of six or eight is joined. A man in the stern of the boats holds the rope of the foremost cow. The rowers then ply their oars immediately . . . The ferrymen are so dexterous that very few beasts are lost.

Incidentally, the 'black cattle' on which this trade was based were named not from their colour or hairiness, but to differentiate them from the beasts kept for milking, the 'white ' cattle. Some Hebridean black cattle – we would call them beef cattle today – ended up walking as far as Smithfield Market in London. By the middle of the nineteenth century the American frontier was being developed, and vast cattle ranches were being established in Texas and elsewhere; many Scots were hired at this time because of their expertise in handling cattle droves, becoming the cowboys of the Wild West. The full history of the contribution of Scots to this aspect of American life remains to be researched and written.

Left: Lochain Dubha near Broadford

Overleaf: Blaven (Bla Bheinn) over Loch Slapin

BROADFORD

THE VILLAGE OF BROADFORD is well supplied with shops, hotels and services; there is a modern hospital, and lots to do. The settlement is rather scattered, taking in some of the crofting townships round about. The old medieval church down on the shore at Breakish is worth a visit. The island offshore is Pabay, intermittently inhabited: it is low-lying and without much in the way of shelter, and while acceptable as a summer getaway home, is not so much fun in the winter; it takes stamina, and character, to survive effectively in such places.

In Broadford there are two roads leading to the south coast. Both are dead ends: one leads to the isolated township of Heaste on Loch Eishort and is not much frequented; the other leads by way of Kilbride and Torrin around the head of Loch Slapin to Kilmarie and Elgol, and is one of the busiest thoroughfares on the island. The limestone quarry at Torrin employs a good number of local people, but most of those using this road are tourists, walkers, climbers and other visitors, perhaps because this is one of the most interesting and attractive parts of the island of Skye. At Kilbride there is the ruin of a medieval church, and at Torrin an 'Outdoor Centre' with hostel accommodation. The view across Loch Slapin is famous and often reproduced; it changes all the time, as clouds and mist gather in the heights of Blaven (in Gaelic, Bla Bheinn). At the head of Loch Slapin there are dozens of shielings, of great archaelogical interest – structures occupied temporarily during the summer grazing season, and which now offer an important insight into a migratory way of life that lasted for perhaps thousands of years.

Kilmarie is in the district of Strathaird or Strath and is one of the centres of Early Christianity on the island. The name is locally pronounced 'Kilvoree', which gives us the clue to its meaning: in Gaelic it was Cille Mharruidh, the 'cell' or church dedicated to St Maolrubha (pronounced 'Maree', more or less) who was as important in the northern part of the Hebrides as St Columba of Iona was in the south. But whereas Columba (in Gaelic, Colum Chille) had the benefit of a brilliant biography written by Adamnan, one of his successors as Abbot of Iona, Maolrubha was not so lucky, and we know almost nothing about him except from place-names, church dedications and fragmentary references in church sources. His main monastery was at Applecross, but there are many traces of him in Ross-shire and on Skye – Loch Maree is named after him because of an island containing another of his cells. He occurs as far south as the island of Islay in the southern Hebrides, within sight of his native Ireland where Kilarrow (pronounced Kila-*roo*) is an early Christian site dedicated to him.

Maolrubha is traditionally supposed to have landed on Skye at Broadford, at Cill Ashig (or ferry). The church near Borline, at Kilmoruy at the head of Loch Eynort in Bracadale is also dedicated to him; an early font from there is in the Royal Museum of Scotland in Edinburgh. And there was 'Maolrubha's fair', on the first Tuesday of September, once known as 'Samarive' which is a corruption of his name; this was an annual event in Portree, where there may have been a chapel in his honour. He appears also to have been honoured at Sartle, near Brogaig in Stenscholl. However, his chief connections are thought to have been with Strath: the stone circle at Kilmarie, Na Clachan Bhreige, hints at the existence of a 'pagan' religious centre there, which perhaps is why St Maolrubha picked it for his Skye base.

St Columba of Iona also visited Skye, at least twice, according to his biographer. Adamnan describes how he disposed of a wild boar which was terrorising the locals from its mountain retreat, and also how he baptised a chieftain 'of the cohort of Geona' who appears to have come from outside Skye and who was buried beneath a cairn at a place then known as Dobur (now Tobar) Artbrannan. Tradition places this spot on the island embraced by the River Snizort, just below Skeabost bridge. This may also have been the site where Columba himself first landed; tradition has it that he built his original church on Skeabost island, and this later became the site of the cathedral or mother church for the whole of Skye. Columba is more associated with the north side of Skye, while Maolrubha is predominant in the southern half of the island; in the eighteenth century the Rev Donald MacQueen claimed there were as many as thirty places of worship dedicated to St Columba in Trotternish alone. While only a few of these are still known, there are still traces of one of the earliest, on what was once an island in the now drained Loch Chaluim Chille ('the loch of Columba') in Kilmuir: here there are remains of beehive cells, surrounded by a cashel (with a little medieval church close by), possibly a monastery founded by St Columba himself.

ELGOL

THE SINGLE-TRACK ROAD winds for fourteen miles from Broadford to the little settlement of Elgol at the end of the road, near the end of the Strathaird peninsula. There is a wonderful and not too demanding walk from here to Camasunary and Loch Coruisk, with matchless views of the Cuillin. There are also astonishing views across to the nearby island of Soay to the west, and to the south-west to the Small Isles of (from left to right) Eigg, Rum and Canna (Muck is hidden). As the midsummer sun sets in this direction, this view has been well photographed – but there is no denying that it is one of the finest in the Hebrides. Film buffs will recognise this as *Local Hero* country: some of the scenes were filmed near Arisaig, on the mainland not very far from the south-east coast of Skye. Bonnie Prince Charlie left Elgol on 4 July 1746, which should appeal to Scottish-American visitors.

2 The Garden of Skye:
the Sleat Peninsula

After the rugged splendour of Blaven and Elgol, Sleat (pronounced 'slate') comes as something of a surprise. Turning off the main road just to the east of Broadford, the road initially crosses fairly uninteresting, boggy moorland, but then it descends to Kinloch to the isthmus between Kinloch at the head of Loch na Dal to the east and Loch Eishort on the west (which takes its name from the Norse for 'isthmus') where the scenery is wonderful; the short spur road over to the crofting township of Drumfearn is certainly worth a detour.

If the rest of the island is the preserve of Clan MacLeod, there should be a sign by the roadside here saying 'You are now entering MacDonald country'. The MacDonalds of Sleat are one of the major surviving branches of Clan Donald, and although not the senior branch of the family, it is they who are entitled to use the title Lord MacDonald (*not*, it should be stressed, the title of Lord of the Isles, which reverted to the Crown in 1493 and is now used by the heir to the throne, amongst whose other titles are Duke of Rothesay and Prince of Wales). The present Lord MacDonald lives in the large house at the head of Loch na Dal; his wife is a renowned writer of books on Scottish cooking, which can be sampled in Kinloch Lodge, now a country house hotel.

At the entrance to Loch na Dal is the tidal island of Oronsay; on the adjacent mainland is the confusingly named township of Isleornsay known by its Gaelic name of Eilean Iarmain (pronounced 'eelan yarman'). It is a beautiful place, and very Gaelic-speaking, largely due to the efforts of its culturally supportive laird.

The road heads inland, but rejoins the coast at Teangue (pronounced 'Tcheng') where you will see Caisteal Camus, or Knock Castle, on the shore of Knock Bay. Its remains date from the sixteenth century, but are fragmentary. It once belonged to the MacLeods, but was taken by force in the late fourteenth century by the expanding MacDonalds. A confirmation of lands to Donald Gorm of Sleat in the early seventeenth century has the proviso that the King should have free access to the castle of 'Camys'. However, when William of Orange sent two warships in 1690, the clan strung up the landing party – understandably since this had already set fire to the chief's main home at Armadale – on gibbets made from their own oars. In fact at

Left: Knock Castle

Pages 34–5: Isleornsay across the harbour with Ornsay on the left

Woods to the east of Ord (Sleat) with the Cuillins beyond

this time the castle was already dilapidated, its fabric being used for building stone at the nearby house of Knock and its adjacent farm buildings. In 1795 the Rev Martin Macpherson described the ruin as 'partly ancient, partly modern, one side being circular and covered with ivy, the other being of the modern style of masonry'; although it is doubtful ·whether the Rev Macpherson ever got very close to the ruin as there is nothing remotely circular about it – it was originally a rectangular keep with courtyard and curtain wall. It is dramatically situated on a headland overlooking the bay, with spectacular views across the Sound of Sleat to the mainland opposite.

At Ostaig a side road turns off and crosses the peninsula to Tarskavaig, Tokavaig, Dun Sgathaich castle (Dunscaith) and Ord, returning across to the east side of Sleat near Teangue. The landscape of Sleat is quite different from that of the rest of the island, being distinguished by tracts of woodland, some very ancient: Coille Dalavil in Gleann Meadhonach and Coill' a'

Ghasgain on the north side of the Ord river, and a smaller wood on the coast of Loch Eishort opposite Eilean Heast come as a surprise after the rather barren landscape of the rest of the island.

It was not always so. The stumps of trees found in bogs in Kilmuir, Duirinish, Strath and elsewhere, and the pollen count obtained from peat samples, prove the existence in earlier ages of birch trees, with some alder, hazel and pine and a few oaks, in areas such as Kilmaluag where they do not now grow. Adamnan in the seventh century and Donald Monro in the sixteenth bear out the tradition that Skye was once well wooded. Monro refers to 'many woods, mony forrests' on Skye and to 'pairt of birkin wood' on Raasay, and describes other offshore islands as wooded. It is probable that the deforestation of Skye began in the Atlantic climatic period when the conditions of westerly winds and excessive rain discouraged tree growth and encouraged the formation of peat. This was in the second century BC; there are many examples of Bronze Age sites, dating from before 1200BC, now partially buried beneath several feet of peat. Deforestation continued during the Scandinavian occupation when much wood was cut down for the building of houses and ships, and over the centuries the woods were a major source of firewood; at one time trees were also cut down to clear the ground and to destroy shelter for wolves.

The most famous piece of ancient woodland in Sleat is the Tokavaig wood, traditionally once a Druid oak grove. It is one of the few natural ashwoods and contains well-developed ash trees, with birch, cherry and hawthorn between. Oaks still grow on the quartzite in the birch wood near Ord, though not on the limestone nearer Tokavaig.

This part of Sleat is thus of great interest to environmentalists and naturalists; but it also contains some of the most important remains of the human history of the island, at Dun Sgathaich (Dunscaith).

DUN SGATHAICH

Dun Sgathaich is probably the earliest of Skye's castles, spectacularly situated on an island stack in the north corner of Ob Gauscavaig, near Tokavaig. The twenty-foot gully between the rocky stack and the mainland was once bridged by a wooden drawbridge; however, the remains of the two arched walls six feet apart are now unsafe. It was originally a Norse castle, and then a stronghold of the MacDonald Lords of the Isles. After the Norse lost sovereignty of the Isles in 1266, it was held by the MacLeods until Sleat was taken over by the MacDonalds; then it became their principal seat until they moved their chief island residence to Duntulm in Trotternish in 1539.

Because of the dangerous access and crumbling masonry it is recommended that this castle should be both viewed and photographed from the mainland.

The views of Dun Sgathaich from the public road are excellent, with the backdrop of the sea, Blaven and the Cuillin. This Sleat 'loop' road is certainly worth the few miles involved, and is best travelled in a clockwise direction.

Dun Sgathaich (Dunscaith) castle and the Cuillins.

*Traditionally Dun Sgathaich was the residence of a warrior queen, who trained men in the fighting arts; the Irish folk-hero Cu Chulainn supposedly journeyed to Skye to complete his military training here. When it belonged to the MacLeods its traditional wardens were the MacAskills, who had held that honour since Norse times. The long and complicated history of this castle has recently been researched in some detail (*The Mediaeval Castles of Skye & Lochalsh, *by Roger Miket and David L. Roberts, 1990).*

ARMADALE

BACK ON THE MAIN ROAD, the Gaelic college Sabhal Mor Ostaig is located on the roadside just where the loop road starts. This is a working educational institution where all subjects are taught in Gaelic, including courses in business studies and media technology. Genuine enquiries are always welcome. There is a small shop selling books and tapes which are not always readily available elsewhere. The college also offers residential courses for Gaelic language learners, and courses in Gaelic music and dance. It has accomplished much in a few years and is still expanding.

Above and below: The gardens of Armadale Castle

A couple of miles down the road is the Clan Donald Visitor Centre, at Armadale – Armadale became the main residence of the MacDonalds of Sleat. Most of their mansion house is now either demolished or a roofless ruin, but a surviving portion of the servants' quarters now contains an excellent exhibition explaining the history of the Lords of the Isles, with an accompanying video; the former stables comprise offices, an excellent restaurant, and a bookshop; while the former estate manager's house has been converted to accommodate a small museum, an extensive library and archives, where ancestor hunters can spend many happy hours on a rainy day.

In the village of Armadale are hotels, craft shops, and the ferry terminal for Mallaig. The view across to Knoydart and Loch Nevis – one of the true remaining wilderness areas in Scotland – is spectacular among the delights of this coastline. The single-track road continues on to Ardvasar, with its old inn, Calligarry and Tormore, ending at the Aird (or Point) of Sleat, where the Small Isles are closer than they were at Elgol but equally impressive scenically.

This part of Skye is very self-contained and has its own distinctive character. The Sleat Historical Society sponsors lectures and excursions, while there are often public events at both Sabhal Mor Ostaig and at the Clan

Left: Armadale Castle

Donald Centre. The gardens at the Clan Donald Centre are immaculately kept, and particularly colourful in the spring, with azaleas and rhododendrons of many varieties. The grounds and surviving ruins of Armadale House give some idea of the Victorian and Edwardian splendour in which the MacDonalds of Sleat lived.

The Tam O' Shanter Dancers (from Canada) at Armadale Castle

EMIGRATIONS

THE HISTORY OF THESE LAIRDS, and their relationship to the people of Sleat, is a mixture of exploitation and charitable benevolence. In the eighteenth century it was very much the fashion for 'improving lairds' to introduce agricultural innovations which resulted in the destruction of a centuries-old communal society, the clearing of population for sheep, a dramatic and unsustainable increase in the island's population, and the emigration of large numbers of people to North America and elsewhere. Lord MacDonald made fortunes from the kelp (seaweed) industry during the Napoleonic wars when the continental sources of alkali needed for soap-making, bleaching, glass-making and other industries were cut off. Kelp was harvested in vast amounts, dried and marketed, making (it is said) from £8,000 to £10,000 a year for Lord MacDonald. The industry collapsed in the early 1830s as continental sources from barilla, a maritime plant growing in Spain, Sicily and the Canaries, became available again.

Emigration was not without appeal to many Highlanders when it was voluntary, and many people became convinced that a better life awaited them in the colonies. In 1769 so many tenants and subtenants left Sleat that Lord MacDonald had to bring in new people from the mainland to maintain the land and run the growing kelp trade. In 1771 a ship took 370 Skye folk to North Carolina; the following winter was a bad one, and encouraged many more to leave. Dr Samuel Johnson and James Boswell were at Armadale in October 1773 during their tour of the Hebrides, and Boswell recorded that the local people performed a dance called 'America' indicating their enthusiasm for emigration; he also remarked:

> Mrs McKinnon told me, that last year when a ship sailed from Portree for America, the people on shore were almost distracted when they saw their relations go off; they lay down on the ground, tumbled, and tore the grass with their teeth. This year there was not a tear shed. The people on shore seemed to think that they would soon follow. This indifference is a mortal sign for the country.

The relatively sudden collapse of the kelp industry around 1830 left a fertile population, enjoying improved living conditions, but largely dependent on the potato. The armed forces provided an outlet for the male population. Sir

Alexander MacDonald of Sleat is reported to have raised 700 men to fight in the American War of Independence, and on the conclusion of their service most of these soldiers, officers and men, returned to Skye bringing home new manners, and knowledge of the wider world as well as money, often in the form of pensions. 'There are among us', wrote the Rev Donald Martin of Kilmuir in the Old Statistical Account in the 1790s, 'many officers of the army who have retired on half-pay, after having bravely served their country – men who possess all those polite and elegant accomplishments by which their profession is distinguished', which reads as if the soldier returning from the wars was welcome in Skye.

Skye probably contributed more men to the forces than any other part of the Highlands of similar extent. Between 1793 and 1805 four thousand were enlisted on the island. According to a report by Glasgow journalist Donald Ross, writing in 1854, by 1837 Skye had provided 21 lieutenant and major generals, 48 lieutenant colonels, 600 majors, captains and subalterns, 120 pipers and 10,000 NCOs and men. Ross also mentioned that by 1837 Skye had provided Britain with two colonial governors, one governor-general, a baron and a judge of the supreme Court of Scotland. And this was at the start of the Victorian era – by the end of the century these figures would have accumulated many times, and the lists of names on the war memorials in the different parishes tell a story of sacrifice for King and country extending far into the twentieth century.

But if island lairds had made fortunes from kelp and sheep, the famine years of mid-century saw them digging deeply into their own pockets to relieve genuine suffering. Lord MacDonald and the MacLeod chief spent almost all their fortunes on famine relief on Skye, and on subsidising emigration which was seen as the only solution, the only way of saving the people from starvation.

As late as 1849 there were still five thousand people on famine relief in Skye. Destitution Boards set up with charitable support in Glasgow and Edinburgh did their best to prevent the Highlands and Islands from becoming another Ireland. A food depot was established at Portree to which grain cargoes were shipped; and relief was distributed in return for work – $1\frac{1}{2}$lb (700g) of meal for eight hours work, with an extra $\frac{1}{2}$lb (226g) for every child under the age of employment and $\frac{3}{4}$lb (340g) for the wife. In 1851 the Skye Emigration Society was founded, with many eminent Victorians offering their support.

In the same year, Alexander Macalister of Torrisdale Castle in Kintyre (of another branch of Clan Donald) bought the Strathaird district of Skye and decided to put sheep upon it. This meant the eviction of five hundred people. While the eight townships of the Strathaird estate were being cleared to make room for the sheep, Lord MacDonald's factor, Ballingall, was evicting the people of Suishnish and Borreraig, the land lying between Loch Slapin and Loch Eishort. The distinguished Scottish professor, Sir Archibald Geikie, describes the resulting scene in heart-rending words:

Black-faced ram, Breakish

Overleaf: Blaven and Loch Slapin

> When they [the evicted families] set forth once more, a cry of grief went up to heaven, the long plaintive wail, like a funeral coronach, was resumed, and after the last of the emigrants had disappeared behind the hill, the sound seemed to re-echo through the whole wide valley of Strath in one prolonged note of desolation. The people were on their way to be shipped to Canada.

Donald Ross wrote to the *Northern Ensign*:

> The scene was truly heart-rending. The women and children went about tearing their hair, and rending heaven with their cries. Mothers with tender infants at their breast looked helplessly on while their effects and their aged and infirm relatives were cast out and the doors of their houses locked in their faces.

Much has been written about the detail of evictions from Highland estates, and the historian of the crofting system, Dr James Hunter, comes from Skye. The factors of the chiefs have often been blamed for brutality in their efforts to build up the wealth of their lairds; or in some cases their desperate and ultimately unsuccessful attempts to preserve their lairds from bankruptcy. Ballingall, Lord MacDonald's factor, has been described as 'notorious', but the difficulties of the chiefs, the tacksmen and the factors in coping with the situation after the 'Forty-Five' – the forfeiture of the estates of those who supported Bonnie Prince Charlie and the problems faced with their eventual restoration in 1785 – were often insoluble.

The depopulation of the straths of Skye to provide pasture for Cheviot sheep continued for years. People were evicted from Bracadale, Duirinish, Minginish: in 1841 the population of Bracadale was 1,842; in 1881 it was 929. From Raasay, 129 people sailed in one day; and 2,000 were said to have been dispossessed on the MacLeod estates. It has been estimated that 6,940 *families* were evicted in Skye between 1840 and 1883, representing perhaps 35,000 people.

From census figures it is thought that the population of Skye at various times was as follows:

1775	11,250 (compiled by Dr Alexander Webster)
1801	15,800
1841	23,000
1881	17,000
1891	15,700
1981	8,500

No society can absorb this rate of change without dislocation and the threat of disintegration, but people living through the problems failed to appreciate their structural nature and tended to deal only with the short-term situation. From a long-term point of view it is difficult to defend the island lairds on Skye or anywhere else.

3 THE ISLAND'S CAPITAL: PORTREE

Portree Harbour

Overleaf: across Portree Harbour

PORTREE is the main town on Skye, and the visitor will almost certainly pass through it, and probably more than once, in the course of his stay. With a population of more than a thousand and a full range of shops and services, it is certainly worth spending the best part of a day there. Nor is it a bad place to spend a night or two – there are often ceilidhs in the local hotels, and other public events and entertainments in local halls. Frequently the best entertainment occurs spontaneously, and there is also a lot to be learned from talking to the locals, or sharing experiences with other visitors. A stroll down to the harbour after dinner to watch the fishing boats unloading is a pleasant way to end the day – though remember that people are working hard there to earn a living, so try not to get in the way!

The new Aros Heritage Centre at present contains an exhibition which includes dramatic re-creations of incidents from island history. Looking at Dr Johnson, one can only feel sympathy for the Highland ponies who transported his bulk during his tour of the Hebrides in 1773! With audio-

visual techniques and sound effects this is a useful introduction to the centuries of Skye's turbulent history. Commentary is available in English, Gaelic, French, German, Italian and Japanese, so there is no excuse for any visitor to claim ignorance of the island's history.

For those with the time or inclination to study local history in more depth, the local public library on Bayfield Road has a good collection of books of local interest, as well as the usual general reading. Several shops sell books of both local and general historical interest.

THE KING'S PORT

PORTREE (in Gaelic, Port an Righ – 'King's Harbour') is so named to commemorate a visit by King James V of Scotland in 1540; before that it was Loch Chaluim Chille, traditionally marking St Columba's arrival point. The power of the Lords of the Isles had been broken with the islands' forfeiture in 1493, but for fifty years thereafter there was a series of rebellions as local clan chieftains sought to fill the power vacuum. So James V decided on a show of force, and took his fleet, with a selection of religious and political personages, on a tour to the Western Isles.

Writing of this voyage in 1655 in his *History of Scotland*, Drummond of Hawthornden wrote:

> This voyage did so terrify those islanders that it brought long peace and quietness to those places afterwards. This active and brave prince not only ventured his life in pursuing and apprehending robbers and highwaymen, which had been neglected in his minority, but his care extended to the most remote islands and rocks of his kingdom; by this voyage he humbled those leaders who thought they might set up for themselves and excerise tyranny over their vassals and tenants. No doubt he had the advantage of the fishing of herrings and other fish in his view which was made more easy when the safest harbours amongst those dangerous rocks were discovered, the dangers and the way to avoid them shown and a full account given of the distances and courses, and the points to which the tides flowed and the times of full sea.

At the time of this expedition the chief of the MacLeods was Alasdair 'Crotach' (hunch-backed) who, though a royal favourite, was forced to give hostages for future good behaviour. One of these was Alasdair's third son, Norman, who accompanied the fleet; it approached by sailing past Duntulm round Rudha Hunish into what was then Loch Chaluim Chille and lairds from the surrounding islands and mainland came to Portree to reinforce their allegiance to their sovereign. In *The Historie and Cronicles of Scotland* Robert Lindsay of Pitscottie, writing in the sixteenth century, made these remarks:

The King passed through the isles and there held justice courts, and punished both chiefs and traitors according to their deserts; syne brought many of the great men of the isles captive with him, such as the MacDonalds and the MacLeods of Lewis etc. Some he put in ward, and some he had in courts, and some he put in pledges for true faith in time coming. So he brought the isles in good rule, and peace, whereby he had great profitable service and obedience of people a long time thereafter.

However, the pacification won by James V did not last long as he died in 1542, throwing the Stewart monarchy into yet another crisis.

CHURCH AND STATE

PORTREE'S place as the administrative centre of the island makes this an appropriate place to consider how both church and state have been organised at various times in the past.

During the Norse occupation Skye was, after 1154, under the archbishopric of Nidaros, now Trondheim, in Norway. The Hebrides remained under Trondheim administratively until 1472, when they were put under the metropolitan authority of the new archbishopric of St Andrews. This was the case even though politically, sovereignty had been transferred from Norway to Scotland in 1266 by the Treaty of Perth. In 1506, after one or two earlier attempts, the Abbey of Iona was erected as the site of the bishopric of the Scottish Diocese of the Isles. By 1561 the Abbot of Iona held lands in various parts of Skye including Armadale and the whole of Raasay and Rona, and claimed the churches of Kilmore in Sleat, Cill Chriosd (Kilchrist) in Strath, and the church at Snizort to which were attached St Moluag's in Raasay and St Mary's at Dunvegan. One-third of the teinds (tithes) of most of these churches were due to the Bishop, including Uig (though this church, Trumpan and St Congan's Glendale were under lay patronage). The MacLeod chieftains retained the patronage of the churches in Bracadale and Duirinish, and claimed (as against the Crown) that of Snizort, until patronage was abolished. Land at Kilvaxter in Kilmuir was owned by the nuns of Iona.

Very few records have survived, and we have little idea how all these changes affected Skye as a whole. From the beginning of the sixteenth century, however, we have records of several appointments in Skye made by James IV in his attempt to establish law and order and get some control over this often reluctant part of his kingdom. Among those appointed was Sir Donald Monro who in 1526 was transferred (or in church parlance, 'translated') to Snizort to which were annexed 'Kilmalowakin' in Raasay and Kilmory in 'Watterness', and who, as Archdeacon of Sodor and the Isles, toured his diocese in 1549 and wrote his famous account of his travels. In

Overleaf: Beinn na Caillich reflected in Loch Cill Chriosd

Pages 56–7: Uig Church

53

1552 Monro was presented to the rectory of Uig. We know from Dean Monro and other sources that the chieftains were not too regular about paying their dues to Iona: James MacDonald, captain of the MacDonalds of Skye, Norman MacLeod of Harris, MacGillichallum of Raasay (in which, of course, Dean Monro had a personal interest) and MacConneill MacNicol of 'Trotarnish' were among those 'put to the horn' towards the end of the century; and in certain cases, their lands were declared forfeit for failing to pay.

Included in Dean Monro's account was a mention of the twelve parish churches on Skye in 1549: Sleat, Strath, Minginish (probably Kilmoruy at the head of Loch Eynort), Bracadale, Duirinish, Kilmory in Waternish (ie Dunvegan), Trumpan, Snizort, Uig, Kilmaluag (later Kilmuir) and Raasay (and possibly one other). These form the basis of today's civil parishes, which were important local government units until recent times: Kilmuir, Snizort, Duirinish, Portree (including Raasay), Bracadale, Strath and Sleat. Anyone doing genealogical research in census records or just wanting to look in the right churchyard for ancestors must know in which civil parish the township they are interested in is located. Otherwise, looking for a needle in a haystack would seem simple by comparison. Confusingly, people tend to use the old Norse district names: Trotternish, Waternish, Duirinish and Minginish, so even locals may not know what parish they live in!

The Protestant Reformation took a long time to affect Skye – as was generally the case in all the islands, although the political activities of the MacDonald chiefs suggests they were already professing Protestants by 1573. The religious wars of the seventeenth century affected Skye as they did everywhere else: it was a confusing time, with episcopacy, presbyterianism and catholicism competing for support in a population that did not seem to be terribly interested – or perhaps was sensibly hedging its bets. In 1700 there were said to be seven Roman Catholic priests and still only seven ministers in Skye.

Throughout the eighteenth century the parish divisions were rationalised, but religion did not become an important issue until well into the nineteenth century. Dissatisfaction with the way in which services were conducted, and resentment at the way the established church chose ministers, meant that at the 'Disruption' of 1843, one third of the ministers and congregations of the Church of Scotland 'seceded', forming the Free Church of Scotland which is still the most powerful social institution in Skye today. These events split communities – and families – and Skye ministers were important on both sides of the national divide.

As a result of the Declaratory Act of 1892, in which the Free Church modified its attitude to the Westminster Confession of Faith, the congregations were again split; the Free Presbyterian church – the 'Wee Frees' – formed at that time remains particularly strong in Duirinish and on Raasay.

In later years the Free Church united with the United Presbyterians to become the United Free Church. But many Skye folk resisted this development, and even after the re-union with the Church of Scotland in 1929, the Free Churches remain strong in Skye, with many adherents and much influence. There are many stories of the fervour of their supporters and the hardships they suffered in preserving their forms of worship, and only by understanding this background can one appreciate the true character of many Skye folk today, especially in the older generation, and their continuing attachment to religious observance.

Nor should it be assumed that these are the strongly held beliefs of a simple people. There is a great tradition of scholarship in the Free Church, and many adherents have gone on to reach the tops of their professions while continuing to be uncompromising in their beliefs. And many people outside the Free Church who find it impossible to agree with its adherents' uncompromising interpretation of things theological, and are irritated by their perhaps over-literal reading of scripture, still sympathise with their desire to preserve their culture, for example by maintaining a strict Sabbatarianism.

All three of the Presbyterian churches in Skye have both English and Gaelic services, and all are well attended. In Portree there is also a Roman Catholic church (St Mary's) and an Episcopal Church of Scotland church (St Columba's), the congregations of which are not large except when swelled by summer visitors.

By comparison, the political administration of Skye is relatively simple, though potentially quite controversial. Before the reorganisation of local government in 1975 Skye was part of Inverness-shire; Portree is 120 miles from Inverness. In that year the Highland Regional Council came into being, covering first-tier functions (for example, education) and encompassing the whole of the north of Scotland from John O'Groats in Caithness to Ballachulish on Loch Linnhe, south of Fort William in part of what had been the county of Argyll. Within this vast area district councils were created to administer a second tier of more localised functions (for example housing), of which Skye and Lochalsh District Council is one.

Current proposals aim to abolish district councils while retaining a single Highland Region with divisional offices offering a degree of accountability locally.

Skye is part of the parliamentary constituency of Ross, Cromarty and Skye, which is basically a way of cobbling enough population together to construct a reasonably viable constituency.

Meanwhile back on Skye itself, life goes on, with the impression that quangos such as the Crofters Commission, Scottish Natural Heritage, the Highland Health Board and the Skye and Lochalsh Local Enterprise Company are just as important as the elected bodies in deciding what happens to the land and the people of Skye.

For the visitor, the most important building in Portree is the Tourist Information Centre, situated in the town's oldest building overlooking the harbour. There is an excellent selection of material explaining the many visitor attractions, and dozens of booklets and leaflets on birds, geology, archaeology, castles, walks, water-sports, craft shops, hotels, guest-houses, camp sites, environmental studies' centres, outdoor pursuits of all kinds, and lots, lots more.

There is a hospital in Portree which was opened in 1964, a new public library building and, most prominently, the island's only secondary school, a rather ugly concrete and glass structure opened in 1971 and badly needing renovation and improvement. Offices for local government functions and quangos are also located in Portree. There is a police station, a Post Office and a modern fire station.

During Skye Week which is usually held in June, there are numerous special events, many of them held in Portree. More masochistic visitors can contemplate entering the Skye half-marathon, over one of the most demanding but scenically most spectacular courses in the country.

THE BRAES

1st batallion Queen's Own Highlanders at the opening of the Highland Games, Portree

THE DISTRICT TO THE SOUTH-EAST of Portree between the main road and the sea, is known as the Braes. Along the minor road which serves this area there are fine views across to the island of Raasay. The Battle of the Braes in April 1882 – often described as the last battle on British soil – was fought between local crofters and a force of sixty police, fifty of them having been sent from Glasgow at the request of Sheriff Ivory of Inverness. Five men were seized, lodged in Portree jail and eventually tried and fined in Inverness.

The cause was, unsurprisingly, threatened evictions and a dispute over grazing rights. The people were provoked by the injustice of the situation and incensed when Sheriff's Officers arrived to serve eviction notices – they were met by an angry mob who forced them to burn the offending documents. When the government's expeditionary force reached Braes it was confronted by a gathering of about one hundred men, women and children, who fought a pitched battle against the forces of law and order with sticks and stones.

The incident caused furious anger throughout Skye and the rest of the Gaelic world. The events were described in graphic detail in all the national newspapers, and depicted in the *Illustrated London News*. The government sent warships to the lochs and troops marched through the disaffected districts to overawe the people. However, wisdom prevailed, and Gladstone set up a Royal Commission to look into the crofters' grievances – there is more information about these events in the discussion of events in Glendale in Chapter 5.

4 CASTLES, FERRIES AND THE OLD MAN OF STORR:
THE TROTTERNISH PENINSULA

THE TROTTERNISH PENINSULA is a 30-mile (48km) long finger of land pointing north from Portree. The interior of the peninsula, which is 5–7 miles (8–11km) wide, is a basaltic lava wilderness, full of strange rock formations; all the traces of permanent human settlement are in a narrow coastal strip.

FLORA MACDONALD

PROCEEDING IN A CLOCKWISE DIRECTION, take the A850 out of Portree, following the signs for the Uig ferry. After five miles you reach the sea at an arm of Loch Snizort, and soon pass the road end for Kingsburgh, where Flora MacDonald, the most famous of her prolific clan, died in 1790. She helped Prince Charles Edward Stuart while he was on the run in 1746, after the disastrous battle at Culloden. Boswell and Johnson met her in 1773: Dr Johnson described her as 'a woman of middle stature, soft features, gentle manners and elegant presence', and was impressed; he thought her name would be 'mentioned in history', and where 'courage and fidelity be virtues, mentioned with honour'.

One of her husband's ancestors was the MacDonald of Kingsburgh who started the island's trade in black cattle with cattle droves in 1502. The upland pastures of Trotternish provided fertile grazing for cattle for four or five months in the year, and are dotted with shielings, the little temporary huts or bothies where families lived during the summer season, largely employed in the production of butter and cheese.

UIG

THE FERRY SERVICE from Uig runs alternately to Tarbert in Harris and Lochmaddy in North Uist, in each case a journey of about 1 hour 45 minutes. Combining the crossing from Uig to Tarbert with the return crossing from

Left: Road near Quiraing

61

HUGH'S CASTLE

A mile north of the bridge over the Hinnisdal River is a farm track down to South Cuidrach, adjacent to Caisteal Uisdean (Hugh's Castle). It is probably the last medieval castle built on Skye, and is regarded as fairly plain and uninteresting by architectural historians, although it is in the usual dramatic coastal setting. The 'Hugh' for whom the castle was named was Uisdean MacGillespuich Chleirich, son of Archibald the Clerk, half-brother of Donald Gorm, the fifth chief of the MacDonalds of Sleat. He was a rascal of the first order, who for fifty years led a life of outlawry and piracy until in 1601 the MacLeods of Dunvegan and the MacDonalds of Sleat finally made peace. As a result of this settlement, Hugh felt able to return to his native Skye, and was permitted to build his rectangular tower at Cuidreach.

However, he planned further treachery against old enemies, to be perpetrated at the house-warming of his newly completed castle. But his plans were unmasked, and Hugh ended his days in a dungeon at Duntulm. According to tradition he was given a platter of salt beef which he demolished hungrily, and a jug, which he discovered to be empty, leading to an agonising death. His bones were displayed in a window of the parish church in the eighteenth century, and eventually laid to rest in 1827.

The Skye Museum of Island Life at Kilmuir, Trotternish

Stornoway to Ullapool makes for an interesting round trip. Caledonian MacBrayne, the ferry operators, offer special 'Island Hopscotch' rates. A more ambitious round trip would be to take the ferry from Uig to Lochmaddy in North Uist, drive south through Benbecula and South Uist (joined by causeways) to Lochboisdale, and take the ferry there back to the mainland at Oban in Argyll.

The ferry terminal at Uig is not a very attractive place to wait, but if you are travelling on the ferry you must be there in good time. There is a waiting room and ticket office but not much else, so it isn't a place to linger.

DUNTULM

THERE IS A MOORLAND ROAD across the peninsula from Uig to Staffin, but the coast road round the north tip of Trotternish is a must, if only to visit Duntulm Castle. This is one of those fairytale Scottish ruins, picturesquely perched on a coastal cliff, and with a history to match.

Just before reaching Duntulm is the burial ground of Kilmuir, which contains a monument to Flora MacDonald. Also at Kilmuir is the Skye Museum of Island Life, a group of preserved thatched cottages illustrating the social history of the island in the nineteenth and early twentieth centuries.

The marauding MacDonalds made Duntulm their chief Skye residence in 1539. It sits on the site of a Norse stronghold, with the strong possibility of an Iron Age fort underneath. Like the Sleat castles, Duntulm was once in MacLeod hands. The striking ruins of the surviving fifteenth-century structure still contain one vaulted chamber at the south angle; a small tower was added in the seventeenth century; and a later house is in the north-west corner of the enclosure. Like all the castles on Skye, it was built

Duntulm Castle and Tulm Island

on an almost impregnable site, with steep fifty-foot cliffs down to the sea on three sides. It had a sea gate as its second entrance, and there are grooves on the rocks below made by galleys. A natural oval mound to the south is known as Cnoc a Mhoid (Moot Hill), where justice was dispensed by the Lords of the Isles.

According to local tradition the castle was abandoned when a nurse-maid accidentally let the baby heir fall from a window onto the cliffs; more prosaically, after the failure of the Jacobite rising in 1715, the castle and Trotternish were forfeited to the Crown. Once renowned as the most imposing castle in the Hebrides, it was quarried for stone for the new MacDonald house at Monkstadt (between Duntulm and Uig), and progressively collapsed; another large chunk fell away in 1990. It is hard now to visualise it as virtually a palace for the all powerful Lords of the Isles, but with a bit of imagination and some study of its fairly well documented history we can begin to get some idea of what it must have been like.

A great ball was held at Duntulm on the eve of the 1715 rebellion, in honour of those setting off to support the Stuart cause. The castle seems finally to have been abandoned around 1732.

TROTTERNISH GEOLOGY

Looking south from Kilt Rock Viewpoint

THE MOST IMPOSING basalt scenery on Skye is the central spine of Trotternish, where the eastern edge of the plateau stands in a high escarpment, the topmost cliffs frowning eastwards over the land between Rigg and Staffin, a broad stretch of the older rocks, of Jurassic age, which were formerly covered by the lava flows. The ridge begins to rise north of Portree and culminates in The Storr at 2,363ft (720m). Swinging slightly northwest, although the crest in general declines in height, the ridge remains the dominating feature of the landscape for nearly twenty miles (32km), mostly over 1,000ft (304m) in altitude and in long stretches over 1,500ft (456m). North from The Storr, Baca Ruadh reaches 2,091ft (637m) and the peak of Beinn Edra 2,006ft (610m).

Along the eastern side of Trotternish the sedimentary rocks below the basalt gave way long ago under the weight above them, and masses of the basalt face slipped downwards in a great series of landslips, one above the other, along the face of the escarpment. These geological events produced the scenery around The Storr, and farther north in the Quiraing, which is as impressive in its way as the majesty of the Cuillins: in front of the Storr lies a jumbled mass of rocks, screes and pinnacles. The Old Man of Storr is a rock

Top left: Old Man of Storr and Loch Fada

Bottom left: The Quiraing: The Needle with The Prison behind

The Quiraing

pinnacle 160ft (48m) high, standing below the 600ft (182m) cliff of The Storr itself; its characteristic outline, visible from Glen Varragill northwards, is also a noted seamark. The Trotternish rock faces are rarely scaled by rock climbers, for basalt is slippery when wet. However, the Old Man was scaled by Don Whillan and James Barber in 1955.

A minor road crosses the ridge from Staffin Bay to Uig, from which one can penetrate into the green heart of the Quiraing, the jumble of

JURASSIC SKYE

The Jurassic rocks of this area include limestones, sandstones and shales. An interesting relic of the time when they were formed – about 150 million years ago – was discovered near the shore at Digg in 1966: a fossil ichthyosaurus, 10ft (3m) in length and the first vertebrate fossil to be found in Skye; though headless, the fossil had most of its vertebrae, ribs and limb girdles. It is now displayed at the Royal Museum of Scotland at Chambers Street in Edinburgh.

Many horizontal sills of volcanic material have been forced between the older strata on the Trotternish lowland as well as elsewhere on the peninsula. One such dolerite sill forms the upper section of the celebrated Kilt Rock, part of the cliffs which plunge into the sea two or three miles south of Staffin Bay.

From the road down the east side of the Trotternish peninsula there are fine views across the sea to the islands of Rona and Raasay, with the hills of Applecross and Wester Ross prominent on the more distant mainland.

strangely shaped hills and rocks that slipped long ago from the precipitous face of Meall nam Suireamach, above and to the west. To the right of the track stand the castellated crags known as the Prison, and farther on is an isolated pyramid 120ft (36m) high called the Needle. Hidden away under the cliff face is the Table, a large, turf-covered, oblong stump of rock about 200 yards (182m) wide, said to have been large enough to hold six regiments of soldiers or 4,000 cattle. The locals used to play shinty there.

5 CLAN MACLEOD:
DUNVEGAN, WATERNISH AND DUIRINISH

Dunvegan Castle

Right: Fairy Bridge, north-east of Dunvegan

IN THE FAR NORTH-WEST of Skye two fingers of land point out into the Minch towards the Western Isles. The small peninsula of Waternish (or Vaternish) is sparsely populated but has one of Skye's most important religious ruins, at Trumpan. The larger Duirinish peninsula has one of Skye's most fertile and beautiful valleys, Glendale – brimming with history, but with hardly a single island family left. The southern half of the Duirinish peninsula is empty, but is renowned for the two flat-topped lava hills known far and wide as 'MacLeod's Tables'. To the south and east of the Duirinish peninsula is the sheltered Loch Bracadale, dotted with a scatter of islands. In the centre of this indented topography of sea-lochs and promontories, nestling in a sheltered, favoured spot on top of an impregnable natural fortress, is Dunvegan Castle, the ancestral home of the Clan MacLeod.

DUNVEGAN

DUNVEGAN is historically far and away the most important castle in Skye, and has been lived in continuously for some seven hundred years. At the head of Loch Dunvegan, it is still occupied by the MacLeod of MacLeod, the chief of the clan. It stands on a promontory, enclosed by the sea on three sides, with a gully to landward. The modern village of Dunvegan is about a mile south-east of the castle. An eighteenth-century view shows a large tower at the north-east angle of around fifteenth-century date, but there were undoubtedly forts on the site going back into the prehistoric past. A new house was built in the sixteenth century with the famous 'fairy' tower between the south angle and the older tower. In the eighteenth century, when the old tower was in a ruinous state, it was replaced by a wing on the west of the sixteenth-century house; later the old tower was restored and linked to the house by an addition with a vestibule and porch, and the whole was finished off in a battlemented 'baronial' style; the gully was bridged and the earlier access on the west abandoned. The castle contains barrel vaulting in the basement, and a pit or prison.

Various treasures may be seen in Dunvegan castle, but perhaps the most renowned is the so-called Fairy Flag which is said to have the power, if invoked, to preserve the clan three times from disaster. So far its power has been called on only twice. In his excellent survey *The Highland Clans* Sir Iain Moncreiffe says it is made of an 'oriental Mediterranean silken fabric, more than a thousand years old, and very carefully stitched in the darns: possibly a saint's shirt kept to bear in peace or war as a lucky relic'. Sir Iain in fact prefers an alternative explanation:

> It sems more likely that it is in fact the famous sacred 'Land-Ravager' flag that King Harald Haardrade ('Hard-Counsel') of Norway brought back from his days as Captain of the Varangian Guard at Constantinople, and which he is known to have left behind with the ships in which the MacLeods' ancestor Godred Crovan (afterwards King of Man and the Isles) escaped after their defeat at Stamford Bridge by King Harold of England in 1066.

Whatever the truth of its origin, there is no doubt at all of its place in the estimation of the MacLeods, who all revere it as their most precious relic.

MACLEOD

The name MacLeod means 'Son of Leod', ultimately derived either from the old Norse word liotr meaning 'ugly', or perhaps more appropriately linked to the Anglo-Saxon leod, meaning 'prince'. In any event, there seems to have been a person named Leod active in the islands in the twelfth century, whose two sons founded the two great branches of Clan Leod: the Siol Tormod and the Siol Torquil.

Anybody with MacLeod connections must make the pilgrimage to Dunvegan, where all the intricacies of the clan's history are explained. The clan charters and archives at Dunvegan are open to researchers (on payment of a fee) and many visitors take advantage of the unusually complete estate papers to do some genealogical searching. There is a restaurant at the castle, and a bookshop, with an excellent selection of literature at all levels to assist in understanding the complexities of twenty generations of clan history.

MACLEOD'S TABLES

*A pleasant story is told of Alasdair
'Crotach' MacLeod, that when
attending a royal banquet at
Holyrood in Edinburgh he was
asked if he had ever seen so
magnificent an entertainment in
Skye. To a persistent lowland
questioner Alasdair eventually
replied that at home he had a finer
hall, table and candlesticks than
anything he had seen at court.
Tradition has it that the King heard
this and decided to test Alasdair's
claim, perhaps during the celebrated
royal visit to Skye in 1540. He was
taken by Alasdair Crotach and his
entourage to the top of Healaval
Mhor, one of the two mountains in
Duirinish known as MacLeod's
Tables. Around the flat surface
stood numerous clansmen bearing
torches which floodlit the scene
while a superb banquet was spread
for the King and his guests.
MacLeod then remarked that the
starry sky was a more splendid roof
than any he had seen in the capital,
and that his clansmen were more
precious than any candelabra.*

CLAN SOCIETY

THIS HISTORY was turbulent and often bloody, with massacres and
outrages seemingly accepted as part of the very fabric of society – an attitude
not unknown in Europe in the twentieth century. In the sixteenth century
Skye, like the rest of the Western Isles and neighbouring coasts, was the scene
of violent struggles between neighbouring chiefs, with rebellions against
central government interspersed with submissions and periods of calm. A
typical example of clan savagery was the massacre of MacDonalds by
MacLeods in a cave on the island of Eigg in which they had taken refuge, in
1577. The atrocity took place in winter; the hideout was given away by
footprints in the snow. A contemporary account describes how the MacLeods
piled brushwood at the entrance to the cave and set fire to it, and 'smoorit
the haile people thairin to the number of 395 persons'.

Revenge for this attack, which wiped out practically the whole population of Eigg, was not long in coming. In the following year, 1578, the

MacDonalds of Uist landed with a force in the bay of Ardmore, in Waternish. They landed secretly from eight vessels, in a fog on a Sunday early in May, and found the people of the district attending service in Trumpan church. With shouts of 'Remember the cave of Eigg!' they set light to the church and burnt up the whole congregation, with the exception of one woman who escaped; although mortally wounded, she survived to alarm the neighbourhood. MacLeod swiftly collected men and succeeded in destroying the invaders in a battle known as (in English translation) 'the Battle of the Spoiling of the Dyke' – the MacDonalds were forced to fight with their backs to a turf dyke; when they had all been killed, this was tumbled on top of them to serve as a burial cairn. The episode is commemorated in a famous pibroch – the classical music of the bagpipe.

Many of the MacLeod chiefs, in spite of their turbulence, were men of high ability and some culture. One was the famous Alasdair 'Crotach' (hunch-backed) MacLeod, a competent soldier, administrator and diplomat possessed of a high degree of culture. He encouraged the clans' bards

MacLeod's Tables and the ruined chapel at Dunvegan

71

CLANS AND REGIMENTS

The clan system prevailed in the Highlands until 1746 when Prince Charles Edward was defeated at Culloden, and central government determined to suppress the clans once and for all and make further rebellions impossible. Draconian measures and equally cruel legislation outlawed Highland dress, made the possession of weapons illegal, and ruthlessly punished any who had supported the Jacobites. The measures were resented bitterly at the time and are still a cause of anger today, but they were effective. The war-like proclivities of Highlanders were put to good use in the King's service in military service overseas, where Highland regiments repeatedly distinguished themselves by their bravery and martial skill.

and treated them generously. He was a patron of the MacCrimmons, and to help the financing of their famous College of Piping he allocated to them the lands of Borreraig and Galtrigil. He conducted himself with ease and grace at court, on equal terms with the great and wealthy lowland nobles.

In the seventeenth century, clan warfare began to die down and the last skirmish to take place between the MacLeods and MacDonalds (barring the occasional Saturday night battles in Somerled Square in Portree after the pubs close) occurred in 1601 in a corrie in the Cuillin known to this day as Coire na Creiche, the 'Corrie of the Raid'.

The clan became an extended family with a paternal chief as its ruler; all members of the clan down to the lowest could claim kinship with the chief. This kinship was not exclusively a blood relationship, for it was common for clans to expand into surrounding territory, or for individuals to join themselves on to a clan, either by marriage or by personal choice.

During the seventeenth and eighteenth centuries the clan system evolved into a more modern system: the chiefs became landlords, but without feudal and judicial powers ('heritable jurisdictions'), and they let their lands on lease to 'tacksmen', generally their immediate kinsmen or heirs, who farmed them or let them out in turn to tenants.

Sometimes the chief let his land on mortgage to a 'wadsetter' who financed the chief's lowland lifestyle in Edinburgh or London, and who only relinquished the land as long as the chief repaid the debt, for example by coming into money by marrying a rich wife.

The tenants often divided their holdings into smaller units which were run collectively as communal townships – the ancestor of the crofting townships of today. The old system was known as 'run-rig', a term better known today for its association with the internationally popular Celtic rock group of the same name, whose members come from Skye.

Highland society in the eighteenth century was deeply affected by the abortive Jacobite risings of 1715 and 1745. It is not generally appreciated that far from being a conflict between Scots and English, these rebellions were in fact episodes in an extended civil war, with probably more Highlanders signed up for the Hanoverian (governement) side than could be persuaded to support and fight for Bonnie Prince Charlie. As is so often the case in civil strife, there were divided loyalties, and divided motives, on both sides.

As far as Skye was concerned, the rising produced much vacillation among the island's chiefs; only the MacLeods of Raasay and their followers gave the Prince whole-hearted support, and that island suffered heavy retribution from government forces. It was only two and a half months after the collapse at Culloden in April 1746 that Skye came into the limelight, with the Prince's landing on 29 June in north Skye, taking his refuge at Monkstadt after a stormy voyage from Uist with Flora MacDonald. In fact the Prince's stay in Skye amounted to no more than six days out of his five months as a fugitive, and one of these was spent on Raasay.

GLENDALE

FOR PEOPLE throughout the Highlands and Islands, the Glendale district of Duirinish will always evoke the resistance of John MacPherson and his fellow 'Glendale Martyrs', who challenged the established social order in the 1880s and were regarded as great heroes during the fight for crofting reform. A series of petty and cruel actions by the local factor (estate manager) decided them to take a firm stand against the continuing erosion of their rights – crofters were even forbidden to collect driftwood from the beach. The purpose of the factor's prohibitions was to force families off the land, but in 1882 the local crofters met at Glendale church and decided to resist further clearances and insist on the reinstatement of those who had already been forced off the land. The authorities despatched a gunboat, HMS *Jackal*, to arrest the ringleaders, some of whom were subsequently imprisoned in Edinburgh. This was one of the more dramatic episodes in a movement throughout the Highlands to make a stand against the landlords and for radical reform, in which many brave men and women took part, including some notable ministers.

In 1883 Gladstone's government set up a Royal Commission to enquire into the conditions of the crofters and their grievances in the Highlands and Islands. Apart from the Glendale skirmish, there was the 'Battle of the Braes', near Portree, which infuriated local opinion; with warships in the lochs and marines marching through the disaffected districts, there was the distinct possibilty of serious civil unrest. However, the appointment of the Royal Commission under the chairmanship of Lord Napier defused the situation, especially since one of its members was Sheriff Alexander Nicolson of Skye and another was Charles Fraser-Mackintosh, the only Gaelic-speaking Member of Parliament and an outspoken radical.

When the Report of the Napier Commission was published – a tremendous source of information about Highland society in Victorian Britain – the general public came to know through the hundreds of pages of printed evidence collected throughout all the crofting counties, of the cruel methods by which a simple folk had been deprived of the land occupied by their families for generations. 'Notwithstanding the studied caution of the language,' wrote Mr Macfarlane, another MP, 'the report discloses a state of misery, of wrong doing, and of patient long suffering without a parallel in the history of our country.'

The passing of the Crofters' Holdings Act of 1886 revolutionised the position, and for the first time in a hundred years the local folk of Skye were treated with justice and fairness. Among other privileges the provision of fair rent and security of tenure was accorded to crofters. In 1887 the Crofters Commission was set up to administer the act, the main points of which were that the crofter received absolute security of tenure, certainty of payment for improvements if he gave up his croft, and certainty that improvements made would not result in increased rent.

GEOLOGY

Geologically the western peninsulas of Duirinish and Waternish are basalt and lava. The basalt produces different kinds of scenery in different parts of Skye: here the landscape is flattish or undulating moorland with occasional upstanding, rather flat-topped hills. The slopes of the moorlands look like gigantic terraces – the geologist James Geikie aptly called them 'corbel-stepped' – and outline the worn edges of successive lava flows. An interesting detail of the lava steps is the existence, here and there, of traces of fossil vegetable matter in sediments between separate flows, indicating the long periods that must have elapsed between successive eruptions.

The highest hills on these western moorlands are MacLeod's Tables in Duirinish: Healaval Bheag reaches 1,601ft (487m) while Healaval Mhor is only 1,538ft (467m). It seems incongruous that the lower of the twin hills dominating this part of western Skye is called Mhor meaning 'big' and the higher is called Bheag meaning 'little', although Healaval Mhor is certainly the bulkier of the two. Both are capped by a remnant of a tough lava sheet whose protection of the surrounding countryside has, through aeons of geological time, been removed by ice and water, leaving the flat tops of which Alasdair Crotach MacLeod was so proud.

Overleaf: Glendale from Glasphein

Before the act, the tenants of crofts had held their ground on what the Napier Commission described as 'an impression indigenous to the country', that they had an inalienable right; this impression had grown out of the ancient clan system and there were no deeds or parchments to back it up. The 1886 Act recognised this 'indigenous impression' and gave it legal status; the Scottish Land Court was set up as an integral part of the reformed system; and in 1912 the Crofters Commission was discontinued and the Land Court operated as an independent corporate body.

However, two world wars and a society in the process of great change meant that further legislation was required. In 1954 a Commission of Enquiry reported on crofting affairs, having been asked 'to review crofting conditions in the Highlands and Islands with special reference to the secure establishment of a small-holding population making full use of agricultural resources and deriving the maximum economic benefit therefrom'. A new act in 1955 re-established the Crofters Commission, to organise, develop and regulate crofting in the crofting counties. It set about its task with such enthusiasm that commentators quickly redefined a croft as 'a piece of land surrounded by regulations' – a definition still valid today. Now, a Crofters Union and increased awareness of the fragility of the crofting way of life seem to have ensured its survival – one part of our society that has benefited from this country's membership of the European Community, now the European Union.

TRUMPAN

TRUMPAN, in Waternish, is said to take its name from its resemblance to a 'timpan', a kind of harp. Trumpan church is on the shore of Ardmore Bay; in its graveyard are two late medieval grave-slabs and a rough stone pillar known as Clach Deuchainn, the trial stone. The hole in this stone was used to test whether an accused person was telling the truth: if he could find it and stick his arm through it without delay while blindfolded, he was innocent, but if he failed and had to grope for the hole in the stone, he was guilty.

Trumpan Church and trial stone

6 WHISKY AND THE CUILLIN RIDGE:
TALISKER AND MINGINISH

THE DISTRICT OF SKYE which lies between Loch Harport and Loch Scavaig is Minginish, the the wildest and least populated part of the island – and certainly the most admired, for this is where the Cuillin hills are to be found.

This is the most dangerous chapter in this book! It cannot be stressed too strongly that the Cuillin are the finest range of *mountains* in Britain, and the most dangerous. These are not hills: they are genuine mountains, and are recognised as such by generations of climbers who, after Skye, have progressed and put into practice in the Himalayas and in other major mountain ranges of the world the skills learned here. True climbers never underestimate the challenge of the Cuillin peaks, but there are hundreds of others every year who do underestimate their severity; some of them die and many more are injured. We would not like you to be one of these, so please do not attempt any of the mountains on your own, or with friends unless you are sure you know what you are doing, are completely confident of your abilities, are properly equipped, and know what to do when things go wrong.

Cuillins across Ob Gauscavaig with Dun Sgaithaich in the centre

THE GEOLOGY OF SKYE

BOTH THE OUTLINE of the island of Skye and the varied landforms of its surface result from the combined effects of rock structure, the moulding of the land by moving ice, and its wearing away by running water. Bold landscape features – large-scale in the central Cuillin mountains, smaller-scale on the northern escarpments and the hills of Sleat – reveal the underlying rocks, and from them geologists have, over the past century and a half, reconstructed the island's physical history and shown that the very striking contrasts in scenery result largely from the differences in the rock structure. Much of the evidence for their theories can be observed, whether on the ground or by examination of maps, by the interested amateur, but every Easter brings teams of university students to Skye, to chip away at the island's rocks with their little hammers and refine our understanding of the detail of the island's geology.

Skye was once part of a much larger land mass, the surface of which was formed comparatively recently, in geological terms, by volcanic activity during the geological period known as the Tertiary – in some cases as 'recently' as 60 million years ago. This took the form chiefly of the intrusion underground of vast masses of igneous rocks accompanied by the outpourings of successive lava flows. The igneous masses, stripped of covering rocks, now stand revealed in the central mountains; the lava flows are now exposed in the cliffs and crags of the escarpments of northern and western Skye. In the upheavals that accompanied this long period of volcanic activity, many faults occurred, initiating lines of weakness which were subsequently attacked by the agents of erosion, both water and ice. Some of the faults coincided with earlier faulting, and many followed the NW–SE or NE–SW trend characteristic of much of north-west Scotland.

The general outline and major surface features of Skye were first fashioned by streams or by the sea, and many hundreds of feet of lava and other rocks were removed during the prolonged denudation of the land before the onset of the Ice Ages. Thereafter glacial erosion exaggerated the island's features, massively etching the Cuillin, rounding and smoothing the Red Hills, deepening and widening the main valleys and opening up the sea-lochs. With the rising sea-level that followed the release of such vast amounts of melted ice, often thousands of feet thick, many fragments around the coast became islands; even Skye itself probably became finally separated from the mainland during this process when the straits on the east were glacially breached and the elongated lochs and sounds which reach in amongst the hills were extended by the drowning of the lower levels of the valleys.

The smoother conical peaks of the Red Hills are apt to surprise the visitor new to Skye, and who has in his mind's eye an image conditioned by calendar photographs of the jaggedness of the Cuillin ridge. They contrast greatly with the Cuillin, both in outline and in colour. The rocks that built them are only slighter younger than the Cuillin gabbro, of a composition

SKYE'S PEAKS

On the road south from Portree your attention is caught by the simple outline of Glamaig, where a steeply tilted flow of basalt lava in fact caps the granite in a summit reaching 2,537ft (773m). Behind it stand the summits of the hills of Lord MacDonald's forest and Marsco, and beyond them the more rugged outline of the Blaven peaks, reaching 3,044ft (928m). To the west of them towers the broken ridge of the Cuillin, seldom without pockets of snow in the north-facing corries.

Top left: Waterstein Head

Bottom left: River Sligachan and the old bridge with Marsco centre right

that weathers to smooth round forms, paler in colour. The granites tend to open up into both vertical and horizontal joints and break down readily into the scree which clothes their lower slopes.

The rocks of which the Cuillin are formed are older generally than those of the Red Hills and are of markedly different composition. They are chiefly gabbro, a coarse crystalline rock that tends to open up into vertical joints – a characteristic that makes these mountains particularly suitable for rock climbing. During the volcanic processes, dark-coloured vertical dykes and horizontal sills, also of igneous material, later forced their way through the gabbro to form features which, when exposed on the surface, diversify it by their different hardnesses in relation to the main rock.

The glacial erosion of the gabbro massif produced a vast amphi-theatre, in the floor of which lies Loch Coruisk. Around its crest sharp-edged ridges, known in mountaineering circles as 'arêtes', are scalloped by high corries which are separated from each other by steeply falling, rocky ridges. The frost-shattered peaks give way to steep-sided, scree-cloaked valleys and gullies. High up on the ice-smoothed rock basins in the corrie floors lie small lochans: a fine example is Loch Coire a Ghrunnda below Sgurr Sgumain in the southern limb of the mountains.

Loch Coruisk itself lies in the heart of the Cuillin in a rock basin that has been gouged out by a glacier, fed from the surrounding corries, to a depth of 126ft (38m) below the present water-level; the floor of the basin is 100ft (30m) below sea-level and its outlet is barred by a substantial ice-worn rock sill through which the Scavaig river has cut a gorge. On rocks near the exit can be seen typical ice-smoothing and striations; perched blocks, left after the ice melted, lie on the surrounding mountain slopes. The Coruisk basin is steep-sided and the loch is typically elongated, as are most of the sea-lochs in this glaciated region. A little farther east, Loch Creitheach lies in a similar, though shallower, rock basin between the eastern limb of the Cuillin and the outlying gabbro peaks of Blaven.

Glen Brittle on the west side of the Cuillin and Glen Sligachan on the north-east are broader valleys but still deep, U-shaped and bearing the marks of glaciation.

The notched summits of the Cuillin are of bare rock. Twenty of them are over 3,000ft (914m) in height and so qualify to be called 'Munros', after the climber of that name who first compiled lists of all the summits in Scotland over that height; the highest, Sgurr Alasdair, reaches 3,251ft (991m). The full grandeur of these mountains can be seen at close quarters only by the mountaineer but impressive views of the range, with Gars-Bheinn on the south seeming to plunge directly into the sea, can be had from Elgol on the east side of Loch Scavaig, or more distantly from the west coast of Sleat, from Tarskavaig or Ord. From this side one looks right into the heart of the Cuillin. Similarly the western ramparts excite the imagination of the climber, in the view from the road between Carbost and Glen Brittle before it drops down into the glen.

BLAVEN

The peaks of Blaven – nearly as much photographed as the Cuillin – stand east of the main Cuillin ridge, closer to the Red Hills. Indeed their dark-coloured gabbro upper slopes give way downhill to granite rocks of a paler colour, for the two types of volcanic rock meet here. Blaven can be seen in all its glory from Torrin, on the east side of Loch Slapin.

Left: Cottage at Torrin with Blaven behind

Overleaf: The Cuillin range

CLIMBING IN THE CUILLIN

MUNROS

Mountaineering for pleasure is a comparatively modern pastime. Little was heard of it before 1850, and it was only from then on that the great ascents of the Alps and later of the Himalayas began. And it wasn't until the year 1889 that the Scottish Mountaineering Club was founded by W.W. Naismith: only then can organised climbing in Scotland, and particularly in the Cuillin, be said to have begun. Between then and 1891 H.T. Munro – later Sir Hugh Munro – listed all the Scottish peaks over 3,000ft (914m): counting subsidiary peaks, there were found to be well over five hundred, and these are known among Scottish mountaineers as 'Munros'. In Skye there are twenty summits of 3,000ft (914m) or more.

THE SKYE MOUNTAINEER B.H. Humble wrote of his native range: 'They are the most notable mountains in Britain and have no equal in all the world.' Coupled with the romance of Bonnie Prince Charlie, it would be fair to say that Skye's other main claim to fame lies in its mountains; they, and particularly the Cuillin range, draw very many visitors to the island, and among these are many serious rock-climbers and mountaineers. For while some of Scotland's mainland mountains offer rock-climbing to the enthusiast, the tops of all can be reached in summer by walkers with the necessary strength and endurance; but in Skye there are many peaks and pinnacles whose summits can only be conquered by rock-climbers.

The earliest recorded climb in the Cuillin was in 1836 when Professor James Forbes – Professor of Natural Philosophy (Physics) at Glasgow University at the astonishing age of twenty-three – made the first ascent of Sgurr nan Gillean with Duncan MacIntyre, forester to Lord MacDonald, as guide.

B.H. Humble pays tribute to one of the very earliest Cuillin climbers: the Rev C. Lesingham Smith. In 1835 he made his way from Sligachan to Coruisk with a forester as a guide, and on the way back they took a different route, doing some rock climbing into Lota Corrie, eventually reaching 'the topmost crag'. 'You are the first gentleman that ever made the pass', said the forester.

Describing the climb, Smith remarked: 'A single false step would have hurled us to destruction and there was very great danger that the first man would loosen some stone that might sweep down the hindmost.' They had to crawl on hands and knees, and Smith found his umbrella, which he always carried on his journeys, 'a sad nuisance'.

In 1845 Professor Forbes returned to Skye after years of work on the study of glaciers in the Alps. It was then that he produced what he termed an 'eye sketch for a map of the Cuchullin Hills in Skye'. This was the first accurate map of the range, with some of the peaks named for the first time. One of the most interesting features of this map is his indication of glacial action, shown by markings south-west of Loch Coruisk and elsewhere on the range.

During 1845 Professor Forbes climbed Bruach na Frithe, but it was not until 1857 that the next notable ascent was made, when Professor Nicol and the poet Swinburne climbed Blabheinn (or Blaven as it is generally written today), that magnificent mountain to the south-east of the main range.

The next mountain to be climbed was Sgurr na Stri – 'peak of strife'; this was achieved in 1859 by C.R. Weld, a member of the recently formed Alpine Club. During his visit Weld also met the then Admiralty surveyor Captain Wood, who drew his attention to the 'Inaccessible Pinnacle', as a mountain never trodden by the foot of man. Weld wrote: 'Surely some bold

The Cuillin Hills from Portree

member of the [Alpine] club will scale this Skye peak ere long and tell us that it is but a stroll before breakfast!' However it was not climbed until 1880, twenty-one years later, by Charles and Lawrence Pilkington.

After Weld's conquest of Sgurr na Stri, no other major peak had its first ascent until 1870 when W. Tribe and John Mackenzie reached the top of Sgurr a' Ghreadaidh. Writing on the nomenclature of Cuillin names in vol xiv of the Scottish Mountaineering Club *Journal*, Mr Colin B. Phillip, close friend of Professor Norman Collie, states that he gathered from dictionaries that the meaning of the name in Gaelic was 'peak of thrashings or rushing wind'. This meaning could well apply to every one of the Cuillin, however, and Professor W.P. Ker insisted that the name came from the Old Norse *greta* meaning 'clear waters'. The Greta (or Ghreadaidh) is the clearest of Skye streams, and 'peak of clear waters' would thus seem to be the most likely meaning of the name.

JOHN MACKENZIE

Many well-known mountaineers have climbed in the Cuillin, among them F.S. Smythe, N.N. Odell, George Mallory and Howard Somervell. These are men whose names have been made famous by achievements in the great ranges of the world, and the fact that they found the Cuillin worthy of their prowess is a proof of the splendour of Skye's main mountain chain.

Among those who have climbed only the Cuillin, John Mackenzie was outstanding; the tributes to him as guide are innumerable. He was born at Sconser in 1856 where his father was a crofter, but the mountains must have been in his blood because in 1866, when he was only ten years old, he climbed Sgurr nan Gillean; and at the age of fourteen he accompanied W. Tribe to the top of Sgurr a' Ghreadaidh. For fifty years John Mackenzie climbed in the Cuillin, both with novices and with experts, and there wasn't a mountain, a corrie, a chimney, or a pinnacle that he did not know. Thousands owed their training in mountaineering to him.

The Cuillin Hills from Elgol

CUILLIN PEAKS IN
ORDER OF ALTITUDE

Feet	(m)	
3,251	(991)	Sgurr Alasdair
3,226	(983)	Inaccessible Pinnacle
3,206	(977)	Sgurr Dearg
3,210	(976)	Sgurr Thearlaich
3,190	(972)	Sgurr a' Ghreadaidh
3,167	(965)	Sgurr nan Gillean
3,167	(965)	Sgurr na Banachdich
3,143	(958)	Brauch na Frithe
3,125	(953)	An Stac
3,107	(947)	Sgurr Mhic Coinnich
3,104	(946)	Sgurr Sgumain
3,089	(942)	Sgurr Dubh Mor
3,070	(936)	Am Basteir
3,069	(935)	Sgurr Dubh na Da Bheinn
3,065	(934)	Sgurr a' Fionn Choire
3,042	(927)	Blaven
3,040	(927)	Sgurr Thormaid
3,037	(926)	Sgurr nan Eag
3,010	(917)	Sgurr a' Mhadaidh (south-west peak)
3,000	(914)	Bhasteir Tooth
2,934	(894)	Gars-bheinn
2,885	(879)	Sgurr Thuilm
2,880	(878)	Sgurr a' Choire Bhig
2,850	(869)	Bidein Druim nan Ramh (central peak)
2,830	(863)	Sgurr na Bhairnich
2,730	(832)	An Caisteal
2,649	(807)	Garbh-bheinn
2,590	(789)	Clach Glas
2,530	(771)	Sgurr Beag
2,480	(756)	Sgurr Coire an Lochain
2,420	(738)	Sgurr Dubi Beag
2,420	(738)	Sgurr na h-Uamha

The next 'first ascent' was that of Sgurr na Banachdich by Sheriff Alexander Nicolson in 1873. Some have argued that the name means 'smallpox peak', pointing out that there are a number of red spots in the rock, while others point to rounded pits in it. But Phillip observes that the rounded pits are found wherever peridotite occurs, and that there is no other reason to connect the mountain with smallpox; he also observes that as there are the rough remains of shielings in Coire na Banachdich, cows were presumably driven to feed there in the summer – and *Banachaig* being the Gaelic for 'milkmaid' he most cogently suggests that 'corrie of the milkmaid' and therefore 'peak of the milkmaid' is not only more agreeable but the much more probable interpretation. Of course, we will never know if a milkmaid ever actually climbed the peak – which seems most unlikely – or if it is named after the lower features.

Alexander Nicolson was probably the most famous of Skye mountaineers. He was himself a Skye man, born at Husabost on the southern shore of Loch Dunvegan in 1827. He was a fine Gaelic scholar, and after taking a degree he made literature his career, being employed as sub-editor of the then current edition of the Edinburgh-based *Encyclopaedia Britannica*; he also worked on the staff of several newspapers. He was called to the Scottish Bar in 1860. He spent his first holiday in Skye in 1865, when he made the ascent of Sgurr nan Gillean with the son of Duncan MacIntyre, who had been Professor Forbes' guide, as his own guide. Of Sgurr nan Gillean, Sheriff Nicolson wrote:

It is undoubtedly a very solemn place to be in, and the slight suggsetion of danger gives it an awful charm. In such places there is no poet whom I would prefer to King David, who, among his other fine qualities, must certainly have been an accomplished mountaineer. If he had not been accustomed to go up and down rocky hills he would not have sung that glorious song:

> 'I to the hills will lift mine eyes,
> From whence doth come mine aid.
> My safety cometh from the Lord,
> Who heaven and earth hath made;
> Thy foot he'll not let slide . . .'

It was in the same year, 1873 that Nicolson climbed the peak which was later named after him, the highest point of the massif which was then known as Sgurr Sgumain, 'the stack peak'. The peak now named after Sheriff Nicolson is 600ft (184m) north-east of what is now Sgurr Sgumain, with the designation of Sgurr Alasdair, the Gaelic form of Alexander. The following year Nicolson succeeded in climbing Sgurr Dubh Mor, probably his most spectacular climb.

In 1880, the Inaccessible Pinnacle was climbed by the Pilkingtons as we said earlier and there followed in the same year the north top of Bidein

Druim nan Ramh, 'the pinnacle of the ridge of oars', by W.W. Naismith, the main top being achieved by L. Pilkington and others in 1883. In 1887 C. Pilkington and party climbed Sgurr Mhic Coinnich, 'Mackenzie's mountain', so called after John Mackenzie 'the only mountain guide of Swiss calibre Britain had ever produced'.

In the same year the same party climbed Sgurr Thearlaich, called after Charles Pilkington, leader of the party; also Sgurr na h-Uamha, 'peak of the cave'; and Clach Glas, 'grey stone'. In 1889 Professor Norman Collie climbed Bhasteir Tooth, 'bhasteir' meaning 'executioner', probably so-called because of its resemblance to an executioner's axe; and in 1896, with another party, Sgurr Coir' an Lochain. Professor Norman Collie has been described as the greatest of all Skye climbers – Sgurr Thormaid, 'the peak of Norman', is called after him. He died at Sligachan in 1942 and is buried in the old churchyard at Struan in Bracadale.

As the separate peaks came to be conquered, climbers began to think of greater feats of endurance. Could the whole ridge of the Black Cuillin, for example, be traversed in a day? For a man to achieve such a thing the great climber G.D. Abraham wrote:

> He would need to have exceptional physique and staying power, to be a quick, skilful and neat rock climber (particularly would he require to be neat, otherwise his hands would be torn to pieces before he got half-way); to posssess an intimate knowledge of the entire range and familiarity with the various difficult sections; while perfect weather, a light rope to 'double' for descents and a carefully arranged commissariat would be necessary.

Mountaineers, particularly Skye mountaineers, were therefore astonished in June 1911 when L.G. Shadbolt and A.C. MacLaren succeeded in covering the range from Glen Brittle to Sligachan between 3.35am and 8.20pm, climbing all twenty major peaks en route, from Gars-Bheinn to Sgurr nan Gillean inclusive. Between 6.07am and 6.25pm when they reached Sgurr nan Gillean, they were never below 2,500 ft (760m). They were actually on the main ridge for just over twelve hours.

As time went on many climbers, including women, performed the feat, so that ultimately the object of the traverse for élite climbers became the conquest of the traverse in less time. One of the most surprising facts about the Cuillin climbs is that, as the years passed, what was at first regarded as impossible gradually became commonplace. The traverse, at first thought beyond the power of all but the most highly skilled, was completed in the 1950s by a young girl of seventeen, who had only three months' mountaineering experience and wore hiking shorts!

We must once again emphasise that for serious climbing, adequate maps, equipment, compass and guide books are essential. Books and maps for climbers are available in specialist shops in Skye and elsewhere.

RALLYING POINTS

Today in Skye mountaineering is not perhaps such a serious matter, or carried out for such serious scientific purposes as in its heyday in the Victorian Age. Moreover climbing has become a far more common pursuit; it is said that on a good day in July one can sometimes see as many as a hundred climbers on the west face of Sron na Ciche, which is believed to be the best mountain for rock climbing. For the mature, whether climbers or not, Sligachan is the best centre for those who have come to Skye for the Cuillin; the Sligachan Inn was always the rallying-point for all the great climbers, and most ventures started there, as many still do. However, probably for most climbing, particularly by the young, Glen Brittle forms the most convenient base, and there is a range of hostel, camp and caravan accommodation there.

TALISKER WHISKY

AFTER A THIRSTY CLIMB – as if any excuse were needed! – it might be a good idea to visit Minginish's other main claim to fame: Talisker Distillery at Carbost – for one thing, there is a wonderful view of the Cuillin from the road above the distillery. At Talisker, Skye hospitality comes in liquid form; you are greeted with a dram of malt whisky, and given time to enjoy it and look at the exhibition of Skye life before going on a tour of the distillery. The guides explain the mysteries of the distiller's craft and keep the visitors amused with local stories. The distillery shop has a selection of single malt whiskies and other gifts.

The whisky produced is a Highland malt; in 1886 the annual output was just over 40,000 gallons – now it is estimated to be 650,000. Barnard wrote of the distillery's situation:

> The Talisker Distillery stands at the foot of a beautiful hill, in the centre of the smiling village of Carbost, which, after the bare and rugged track we had passed through [they had driven from Portree and Sligachan] was an agreeable change, and seemed quite a lively place. On the broad slopes of the hills, which were covered with crofters' holdings, husbandmen were busy tilling the soil; while at the Distillery below and the village which surrounds it, all was life and motion. Driving along we were struck with the picturesque situation of the Distillery, which stands on the very shore of Loch Harport, one of the most beautiful sea-lochs on this side of the island.

Dr Samuel Johnson visited Talisker House in 1773, and was impressed:

> . . . the place beyond all that I have seen from which the gay and the jovial seem utterly excluded, and where the hermit might expect to grow old in meditation, without possibility of disturbance or inter- ruption. It is situated very near the sea, but upon a coast where no vessel lands, but when it is driven by a tempest on the rocks. Towards the land are lofty hills streaming with waterfalls. The garden is sheltered by firs, or pines, which grow there so prosperously that some, which the present inhabitants planted, are very high and thick.

This passage captures well the spirit and remoteness of the place. Talisker House was traditionally in the ownership of the son of the MacLeod chief.

Talisker whisky is described today as 'heavily peated' – though not so heavily as some of the Islay malts for instance. Much, but not all, of the peat used in the process is local; Barnard describes how he saw women digging and bringing in the fuel. Like all other whiskies, whether malt or grain, Talisker is colourless – it derives its final amber hue from the sherry casks in which it

ORIGINAL DISTILLERY

The only distillery on Skye was put up in 1830 by the brothers Hugh and Kenneth Macaskill, who were sheep farmers. They were granted a lease of the ground by the MacLeod chieftain. The original plant (as described vividly by Alfred Barnard in his book The Whisky Distilleries of the United Kingdom, published in 1887 and since reprinted) was still functioning in 1960, when a disastrous fire forced much rebuilding; however, this did give the opportunity for substantial modernisation. The distillery is still manually operated as far as the malting process is concerned, and is one of the very few distilleries left which are not automatic. One of the most striking things to anyone visiting Talisker Distillery is the gleaming copper of the stills.

Left: Talisker Distillery still-house

Right: Dun Ardtreck, near Carbost

Talisker Bay

Talisker Point

is left to mature. The peating and maturing in sherry casks are part of the process which gives Talisker its distinctive flavour. The whisky has to be matured for three years before it can be sold legally as 'Scotch whisky'; in fact the most usual period for maturing is eight to ten years, and sometimes it is kept for fifteen to twenty years. The increase in quality is reflected in the price.

Most of the output of this distillery goes to be blended, but some is bottled as true Highland malt whisky. As such, no connoisseur would drink it other than neat, and no true Scotsman would refer to it vulgarly as 'Scotch'. There is a school of thought that believes a malt whisky benefits from the addition of a few drops of local water – any other additive is considered to diminish the experience.

TALISKER GEOLOGY

BASALT GEOLOGY can be explored in Minginish: the hills form massive terraced slopes that reach the western coasts of the district in cliffs as high as 900ft (274m) in places, and spectacular waterfalls tumble off the terraces into the sea. Carbost is a likely centre for expeditions: Minginish is not as well provided with access roads as other parts of Skye, and so some planning and forethought is required when exploring. Some of this district is best viewed from the sea. Several of the tabular tops reach 1,300–1,400ft (396–426m), and apart from the river mouths there is very little land below 100ft (30m) in altitude. Behind Talisker Bay the crags of Preshal More stand up in basalt columns. Farther east, on the steep hillsides east of Loch Eynort and west of Glen Brittle, are the most extensive areas of forested land on Skye, overshadowed by the neighbouring Cuillin.

7 OVER THE SEA TO RAASAY:
MORE MacLEODS AND A GREAT POET

Dun Caan, Raasay, the high point of the island, on which James Boswell danced a jig while touring the Hebrides with Dr Johnson (Norman Newton)

The pier at Raasay, looking across to the mountains of Skye (Norman Newton)

IT IS CERTAINLY POSSIBLE to spend an entire holiday on Raasay, and many lucky people do; but for the purpose of this book we shall assume that visitors are only going across for the day and so have limited time and opportunities.

The island of Raasay lies east of Skye, separated from the Trotternish peninsula by the Sound of Raasay. The mainland district of Applecross is 8 miles (12.8km) to the east. Raasay is 13 miles (21km) long and up to 3miles (5km) wide, with a population of 180. It is a hilly island, rising in the centre to the flat-topped Dun Caan (1,456ft; 444m) where Boswell 'danced a Highland dance' in 1773.

There is a short ferry connection to Sconser on the south side of Loch Sligachan, on the main road from Broadford to Portree; note that there is *no* Sunday service. Raasay is a bastion of the Free Church which has strong Sabbatarian beliefs, and which visitors are asked to respect. The principal settlement is Inverarish, between the ferrry slip and Raasay House; the latter is where the MacLeod laird, his wife and large family (three sons and ten daughters) entertained Boswell and Dr Johnson in lavish style. They expressed in rather flowery prose what generations of visitors to the Hebrides have felt; 'Such a seat of hospitality amid the winds and waters fill the imagination with a delightful contrariety of images'! Raasay House stands on the site of a tower house built in 1549.

The original Raasay House was burned by government troops after Culloden; because the outlawed Bonnie Prince Charlie was given refuge on Raasay, 300 houses were burned, 280 cows and 700 sheep were slaughtered, several horses shot, and most of the island's boats were holed and sunk.

After John MacLeod of Raasay sold the island in 1843, it passed through the hands of numerous owners, none of whom was able to reverse the trend of emigration, depopulation and poverty which continued until recent times. Raasay House was run as a hotel from 1937 to 1960, after which it was allowed to collapse into a dilapidated ruin. However, it is now used as the base for an excellent outdoor adventure school. There is a range of accommodation facilities on Raasay, including a hostel, bed-and-breakfast houses and a hotel; but in the summer season it is usually necessary to book well in advance. Details are available from the Tourist Information Centre in Portree.

On the east side of the island is Brochel Castle, built by the MacLeods of Lewis in the fifteenth century. It is built on volcanic rock, its only entrance being from the east, approached by a steep narrow ridge; it is now very ruinous, not to say dangerous, and should *not* be approached too closely. In particular the walls are in a very crumbly and unstable condition and should not be climbed upon. The last MacLeod of Raasay chief to live at Brochel was the famous Iain Garbh ('Mighty John'), a man of reputedly prodigious strength who succeeded his father Alexander in 1648. He was greatly venerated by his tenants, and with his death it seems that there was a vacuum in the succession until his cousin Alexander became chief in 1692. Thereafter, if not before, the chief residence was at Clachan, where Raasay House is now located. The story of how Brochel Castle was built, in tragic circumstances, can be read in *The Mediaeval Castles of Skye & Lochalsh*, by Roger Miket and David L. Roberts (1990).

The two miles (3.2km) of road joining Brochel to Arnish are known as 'Calum's Road' and is the work of one man, Calum MacLeod, who died in 1988 soon after building it single-handed over a period variously estimated at ten to fifteen years. With just a pick and shovel and a wheelbarrow, and a manual of road-making which cost him 3s (15p), he decided to build the road himself after the local council had turned down his requests for a proper access to his home. Raasay Community Council decided to honour his achievement with a cairn, which was unveiled in 1990, with a suitable plaque in Gaelic and English.

Raasay has an iron ore mine which was operated by German prisoners of war during World War I. The processing plant can still be seen, and also the course of a quarry railway, although most of the machinery was removed for scrap in the 1920s. It is possible to view the entrances to the quarry tunnels, although going inside the old mines is not recommended.

A GREAT POET

Raasay is the native island of the poet Sorley Maclean, who writes in his native language, Gaelic, as well as in English. His work is highly regarded internationally and he is often described as Britain's greatest living poet. His name in Gaelic is Somhairle MacGill-Eain ('Somerled, son of the servant of John') and his renown has helped to revive 'Sorley' as a personal name in Skye and other Gaelic-speaking areas. His brother Calum, who died in 1960 at the age of forty-five, was the author of The Highlands, *one of the most evocative and perceptive accounts of the Highlands ever written. Sorley Maclean was born in 1911, in the township of Osgaig, near which a cairn has been built in his honour. In subject his poems range from the horrors of war in the North African desert to the landscapes and woods of Skye and Raasay. His poem* Hallaig *was described in* The Scotsman *as a 'passionate lament for a lost society which lives on only in the poet's mind, a poem in which a whole culture gathers itself for a definitive statement'. The walk from the road end at North Fearns along the old track to the Hallaig Woods, then perhaps back over Dun Caan to Raasay House, is a fine half-day excursion.*

8 WALKS AND EXCURSIONS

AS MENTIONED in our description of the Cuillin, the mountains of Skye are to be treated with respect. We do not propose to offer any guidance as to mountaineering, since there are many excellent specialist books available: for reasons of safety, anybody seriously interested in ascending any of the Cuillin peaks would do well to study these. However, as a taster, we offer a few less strenuous excursions as examples of the range of possibilities for the walker and rambler on Skye.

ACCESS

FIRSTLY, in order to ensure that you have a rewarding and trouble-free visit to Skye, a brief word about rights of access. Basically, access to the countryside in Skye, and to all historic sites, is unrestricted, bounded only by considerations of courtesy and common sense. It is sensible to ask for directions, if not for permission. Any advice offered should be followed, and visitors should take particular care not to damage dykes and fences, and to avoid disturbing stock, especially in the lambing season.

Artist painting Loch Pooltiel from Glendale

Freedom of access does not give visitors the right to tamper with historic sites, without the owner's permission. Visitors must also apply to the appropriate estate for permits to fish. Hotels and the Tourist Information Centre can offer advice about where to apply: on some lochs boats are available. The same applies to anybody wishing to fish for salmon or to shoot game. Doing these things without permission is poaching, and illegal.

So, although there are no laws prohibiting rights of access, there has to be some give and take with landowners and farmers. Their livelihood is often at stake, as well as other people's jobs. From the point of view of personal safety it is reckless to go hill-walking on big shooting estates during the shooting season. Again, the estate offices can advise if any shooting parties are likely to be on the hills.

Left: across Loch Pooltiel near Meanish Pier

Overleaf: Staffin Bay from the Quiraing

EQUIPMENT

Visitors always hope for good weather, but in our climate there are no guarantees, only wishful thinking, and in the absence of a direct line to the Almighty certain precautions are essential. The key elements in Skye's weather are wetness and wind. Even when the sky is blue and the lochs are shimmering with scenic beauty, the ground underfoot is likely to be boggy once off roads and tracks. Adequate raingear and correct footwear will make it possible to have a good time, whatever the weather; inadequate protection leads inevitably to saturation, cold, misery, recriminations and regret. Wet clothing can be dried out – eventually – but without doubt prevention is better. Even on a fine day there is likely to be a brisk breeze, and light, windproof jackets or anoraks should always be carried. The weather can change quickly, and although inadequately clad walkers are unlikely to come to any harm, they can certainly become exceedingly miserable very quickly. Climbers have to take special precautions – some of these were outlined in Chapter 6.

Correct footwear is most important. Proper walking boots with Vibram soles are best, and need not be expensive or heavy. Good walking shoes are acceptable only for farm tracks or beachcombing expeditions. Trainers will become soaked in anything but drought conditions and can be ruined quickly and easily. Wellies are uncomfortable to walk in for any distance, and are positively dangerous in wet conditions. If you buy new boots or shoes for your island adventure, try to break them in first, or come well provided with plasters to deal with the inevitable blisters.

QUIRAING

THIS WALK is quite demanding and requires a reasonable degree of fitness, but it is hard to imagine more dramatic scenery in only 4 miles (6.5km). The weird geological formations in this area were described in Chapter 4. To reach them, drive 19 miles (30km) north of Portree on the A855. From Brogaig, just north of Staffin, take the single-track road to Uig, and park in the car park after 2½ miles (4km). The car park is on the south side of the road.

Cross the road and follow the well-defined track along the base of the cliffs. After 1 mile (1.6km) you will see some of the well-known rocky features on isolated rocky knolls on the far side of a rough valley: the Prison, the Needle and the Table. If you are visiting in the summer months, you will not be alone.

From the Table, continue for just under a mile, through a stone dyke, until you reach the lowest point of the ridge on your left. Scramble up on to it and make your way back along the tops of the cliffs. There is a spectacular view from the top of Meall na Suiramach. Continue along the top of the cliffs and return to the car park.

MIDGES

Little can be done about midges. Some people think they are sent by Divine Providence as a punishment, and when you are suffering because of them this seems the only possible explanation. Local shops sell various potions and preparations which, it is claimed, repel midges and some of these give a measure of short-term protection. The best protection against midges is wind, which fortunately is not in short supply on Skye. So when seeking out a picnic spot or campsite, stay away from damp sheltered locations.

Left: Uig from the road north

Overleaf: Beinn na Caillich reflected in Loch Cill Chriosd

PORTREE

THIS IS AN EASY WALK, but can be damp in places. The scenery along the coast is outstanding and there are good views of Portree. It is about 2¹/₂ miles long (4km). From the town centre, make your way around the north side of Portree Bay. Keeping to the right at two junctions, continue until you reach a parking area and take the path to the right, signposted 'jetty'. Follow this path to a viewpoint and flagpole commemorating the Nicolson clan, then continue round the steep headland. Just round the point of the headland go through a gate in the stone dyke and continue until you reach a fence. Turn left along the fence until you come to a gate: go through this and cross the field, then cross a stile and climb up the slope beyond to a track, and turn left.

This track leads to the houses at Torvaig. Follow the track past the house to the left, heading downhill towards two large farm buildings. Go between these and continue across moorland until you reach another stile. Cross the stile into an area of woodland and continue downhill to the road and make your way back into Portree.

ELGOL

THIS WALK is quite demanding in places, and is about 9 miles (14.5km) long. It starts from the car park in Elgol, which is 14 miles (23km) south of Broadford along the winding B8083. From the car park, walk back up the road for a short distance, then turn left along a track behind some houses, signposted for 'Garsbheinn'. Beside the last of these houses there is a sign for the path to Coruisk.

Follow the Coruisk path, which is well-defined but quite steep in places, for a little over 3 miles (4.8km) to the bay at Camusunary. The coastal scenery is fantastic, with views across Loch Scavaig to the jagged peaks of the Cuillin range and the island of Soay. It is best done on a clear day. If it has been raining, crossing the burn at the foot of Glen Scaladal can be a bit tricky.

The shortest way of returning to Elgol is to retrace your steps, but as an alternative follow the clear track from Camusunary up the south side of Abhainn nan Lean over the hills to the east until it joins the B8083. Turn right for the 3¹/₂ mile (5.5km) walk back along the road to Elgol.

POINT OF SLEAT

AN EASY WALK for 4 miles (6.5km) along a clear track, rewarded by good coastal scenery. To start the walk, drive down the Sleat peninsula to Armadale, then continue straight on for another 5 miles (8km) to the end of the public road at the church at Aird of Sleat. Take care not to block entrances when parking, as there is not a separate car park.

Go through the gate at the end of the public road and follow it across an area of heather moorland and down to the tiny natural harbour. A short scramble over the rocks to the left of the harbour is rewarded with fine views south, to the islands of Eigg and Rum.

You can add another 1¹/₂ miles (2.5km) to this walk by following a rough track from the harbour over moorland to the Point of Sleat lighthouse. Return to Aird of Sleat by the same route.

Overleaf: Cottage at Luib

HALLAIG (RAASAY)

THIS WALK is about 5 miles (8km) long, and is, for the most part, along well-defined tracks, but it involves a little scrambling at points where the path has deteriorated or disappeared. The island of Raasay was described in Chapter 7. From the pier, follow the road to the village of Inverarish, then turn right and drive across the island to the townships of North and South Fearns. Park just beyond the last house on this road, then follow the old road to Hallaig. Just before the track descends to the abandoned township there is a cairn honouring the poet Sorley Maclean and 'the people of Hallaig and other crofting townships'.

Take time to explore the old settlement, and reflect on this aspect of Highland history – there are hundreds of places like this throughout the Highlands and Islands.

You can return to North Fearns either along the same route, or follow the Hallaig Burn up to its watershed and continue along a rough path by the side of Beinn na Leac until the path finally fades away – but by this time you should be able to see the public road ahead. Turn left at the road to return to your starting point, or if you want to walk back to the pier, turn right.

Spear thistle

USEFUL INFORMATION AND PLACES TO VISIT

TOURIST INFORMATION CENTRES

Tourist Information Centre,
Bayfield House, Bayfield Road, Portree, IV51 9EL
Accommodation bookings, leaflets, books, maps.
Tel: 01478 612137; Fax: 01478 612141. Open all year.

Seasonal Information Centres in Broadford and Uig, open April to September.

FERRY SERVICES

Caledonian MacBrayne, Armadale (for Mallaig).
Tel: 01471 844248; Fax: 01471 844212.
Vehicle reservations are essential for the Mallaig-Armadale crossing.

Caledonian MacBrayne, Uig (for Western Isles).
Tel: 01470 542219; Fax: 01470 542387.

Glenelg-Kylerhea ferry, Mr R. MacLeod.
Tel: 01599 511302; Fax: 07070 600845.
Operates from Easter to late October.

PLACES TO VISIT

An Tuireann Arts Centre, Portree.
Exhibitions, café, disabled access. Tel: 01478 613306.

Aros Heritage Centre, Viewfield Road, Portree.
Dramatic recreations of island history, with multi-lingual headsets. Restaurant and bookshop. Open all year, 9.00am–9.00pm (low season, 9.00am–6.00pm).
Tel: 01478 613649; Fax: 01478 613100.

Borreraig Park Exhibition Croft, Glendale.
A display of locally found artefacts and implements.
Tel: 01470 511311.

Brochel Castle (ruin), Raasay.
Built by the MacLeods of Lewis in the fourteenth century; in a highly dangerous state.

Caisteal Camus, or Knock Castle (ruin), Sleat
Ancient stronghold of the MacDonalds of Sleat.

Castle Moil (ruin), Kyleakin
Ancient seat of the MacKinnons, near the ferry slip at Kyleakin.

Clan Donald Visitor Centre, Armadale
Museum of the Isles exhibit tells the history of the MacDonald Lords of the Isles. Family history records. Restaurant and bookshop. Open daily, 9.30am–5.30pm, Easter to end of October; restaurant open until 8.30pm, July–August.
Tel: 01471 844227; Fax: 01471 844275.

Colbost Folk Museum, near Dunvegan
Nineteenth-century thatched cottage.
Tel: 01470 521214.

Dun Sgathaich Castle, or Dunscaith (ruin), Sleat
Skye's oldest castle, a MacDonald stronghold until 1539.

Duntulm Castle, (ruin)
One of the most important fortresses of Clan Donald.

Dunvegan Castle, Dunvegan
Open from March to October, seven days a week, admission charged. The home of MacLeod chieftains for 800 years. Clan exhibition, archives, bookshop, restaurant. Tel: 01470 521206.

Giant Angus MacAskill Museum, Dunvegan
Illustrating the life and achievements of the tallest Scot of them all. Tel: 01470 521296.

Luib Folk Museum, near Broadford
Thatched cottage with 'The Trail of the Fugitive' exhibition in honour of Bonnie Prince Charlie.
Tel: 01471 822427.

Raasay House, Raasay

An eighteenth-century laird's house, now housing Raasay Outdoor Centre and a small heritage museum of local history. Tel: 01478 660266.

Sabhal Mor Ostaig, An Teanga, Sleat

Gaelic college offering courses in Gaelic language, music and culture. Tel: 01471 844373.

Skye Environmental Centre, Harrapool, Broadford

Informative displays on the geology and natural history of Skye and home of the International Otter Survival Fund. Tel: 01471 822487.

Skye Museum of Island Life, Kilmuir

Group of preserved thatched cottages illustrating the social history of the island over the last two hundred years. Tel: 01470 552319.

Skye Serpentarium, The Old Mill, Harrapool, Broadford

Reptile exhibition, irresistible to children. Tel: 01471 822209.

Talisker Distillery, Carbost

Guided tours. Open April to October, Mon–Fri, 9.30am–4.30pm; November to March, Mon–Fri, 2pm–4.30pm. Tel: 01478 640314.

Toy Museum, Holmisdale House, Glendale.

A hit with kids, and a chance to relive your childhood. Tel: 01470 511240.

There are numerous craft shops, galleries, outdoor centres and activity centres throughout Skye – details of current possibilities are published annually by the Local Tourist Board.

Further Reading

Cooper, Derek. *Skye* (Queen Anne Press, 1989)

Ferguson, M. *Rambles in Skye* (Irvine, 1885)

Humble, B. H. *The Cuillin of Skye* (London, 1952)

MacCulloch, J. A. *The Misty Isle of Skye* (Eneas Mackay, 1927)

MacDonald, Jonathan. *Discovering Skye* (1993)

MacLean, Sorley. *Spring Tide and Neap Tide: selected poems 1932–72* (Canongate, 1981)

Macpherson, Duncan. *Gateway to Skye* (Eneas Mackay, 1946)

Martin, Martin. *A Description of the Western Islands of Scotland* (1695)

Miket, Roger and Roberts, David L. *The Mediaeval Castles of Skye & Lochalsh* (MacLean Press, 1990)

Nicolson, Alexander. *History of Skye* (MacLean Press, first published 1930, revised edition 1994)

Sillar, Frederick C. and Meyler, Ruth M. *Skye* (David & Charles, 1973)

Smith, A. *A Summer in Skye* (London, 1865)

Swire, O. F. *Skye, the Island and its Legends* (Glasgow, 1961)

PLACE-NAMES AND THEIR INTERPRETATION

Armadale	N. *armr-dalr*	bay valley
Boreraig	N. *borgar-vik*	fort bay
Bracadale	N. *brekka-dalr*	slope-valley
Broadford	N. *breida-fjord*	broad firth
Carbost	N. *Kari-bolstadr*	Kari's township
Cuillin	G. *cuilionn*	like holly, jaggy
	G. *cu Chulainn*	the hound of Culann
Digg	G. *dig* (pron 'jig')	dyke, or ditch
Druimfearn	G. *druim fhearna*	ridge of the alder
Duirinish	N. *dyr-nes*	deer headland
Dun Grianan	G. *dun grianan*	sunny fort
Duntulm	G. *dun*; N. *holmr*	fort of the islet
Dunvegan	G. *dun*; N. *Bekan*	fort of Bekan
	G. *dun bheagain*	fort of the few
Elgol	G. *fal a'ghoill*	enclosure of the stranger
Fairy Bridge	G. *beul ath nan tri allt*	ford of the three burns
Flodigarry	N. *floti-gardr*	fleet enclosure
Glendale	G. *gleann*; N. *dalr*	the glen valley
Hallaig	N. *heilag-vik*	holy bay
Harlosh	G. *charr lois*	rock of the fire
Harport	N. *hafra-fjord*	he-goat firth
Idrigill	N. *ytri-kollr*	outer hill
Kensaleyre	G. *ceann-sal*; N. *eyrr*	sea-end gravel beach
Kilmaree	G. *cill Maolrubha*	St Maolrubha's church
Kilmuir	G. *cill Moire*	Mary's church
Kyleakin	G. *caol*; N. *hakon*	the kyle (sound) of Hakon

Loch Eishort	N. *eiths-fjord*	isthmus firth
Loch Eynort	N. *Einar-fjord*	Einar's firth
Loch Snizort	N. *snaes-fjord*	snow firth
Minginish	N. *megin-nes*	main headland
Monkstadt	N. *munkr-setr*	monk's seat, residence
Ornsay	N. *orfiris-ey*	ebb-tide island
Ostaig	N. *ost-vik*	east bay
Portnalong	G. *port na long*	port of the ship
Portree	G. *port-an-righ*	the King's port
Raasay	N. *raa-s-ey*	roe-deer island
Shulishader	N. *sule-setr*	gannet sheiling
Skeabost	N. *Skidi-bolstadr*	Skidi's township
Skulamus	N. *Skulimus*	Skuli's moss
Skye	G. *an t-Eilean Sgiathanach*	the winged island
Sleat	N. *sletta*	a plain, level area
Sligachan	G. *slige-ach-an*	shelly place
Staffin	N. *staffr*	column (geological)
Storr	N. *storr*	dominant
Strathordil	G. *srath*; N. *svordr-dalr*	grassy pasture glen
Strolamus	N. *Sturli-mus*	Sturli's moss
Talisker	G. *t*; N. *hallr-sker*	the sloping rock (skerry)
Tarskavaig	N. *thorskr-vik*	cod bay
Trotternish	N. *Throndar-nes*	Thrond's headland
Uig	N. *vik*	bay
Waternish	N. *vatrs-nes*	watery headland

G. – Gaelic
N. – Norse

INDEX

Page numbers in *italic* indicate illustrations